PREFACE

The first edition of this book appeared in October, 1918, a few weeks before the signing of the Armistice, when the United States was at the high tide of its power and influence. In view of the subsequent course of events, some of my readers may question the propriety of the original title. In fact, one of my friends has suggested that a more appropriate title for the new edition would be "From Isolation to Leadership, and Back." But I do not regard the verdict of 1920 as an expression of the final judgment of the American people. The world still waits on America, and sooner or later we must recognize and assume the responsibilities of our position as a great world power.

The first nine chapters are reprinted with only a few verbal changes. Chapter X has been rewritten, and chapters XI and XII have been added.

JOHN H. LATANÉ.

Baltimore, June 10, 1922.

CONTENTS

CHAPTER

I. ORIGIN OF THE POLICY OF ISOLATION II. FORMULATION OF THE MONROE DOCTRINE III. THE MONROE DOCTRINE AND THE EUROPEAN BALANCE OF POWER IV. INTERNATIONAL COOPERATION WITHOUT THE SANCTION OF FORCE V. THE OPEN-DOOR POLICY VI. ANGLO-AMERICAN RELATIONS VII. IMPERIALISTIC TENDENCIES OF THE MONROE DOCTRINE VIII. THE NEW PAN-AMERICANISM IX. THE FAILURE OF NEUTRALITY AND ISOLATION X. THE WAR AIMS OF THE UNITED STATES XI. THE TREATY OF VERSAILLES XII. THE WASHINGTON CONFERENCE INDEX

From Isolation to Leadership

I

ORIGIN OF THE POLICY OF ISOLATION

The Monroe Doctrine and the policy of political isolation are two phases of American diplomacy so closely related that very few writers appear to draw any distinction between them. The Monroe Doctrine was in its origin nothing more than the assertion, with special application to the American continents, of the right of independent states to pursue their own careers without fear or threat of intervention, domination, or subjugation by other states. President Monroe announced to the world that this principle would be upheld by the United States in this hemisphere. The policy of isolation was the outgrowth of Washington's warning against *permanent* alliances and Jefferson's warning against *entangling* alliances. Both Washington and Jefferson had in mind apparently the form of European alliance common in their day, which bound one nation to support another both diplomatically and by force in any dispute that might arise no matter whether it concerned the interests of the first state or not. Such alliances were usually of the nature of family compacts between different dynasties, or between different branches of the same dynasty, rather than treaties between nations. In fact, dynastic aims and ambitions were frequently, if not usually, at variance with the real interests of the peoples affected. It will be shown later that neither Washington nor Jefferson intended that the United States should refrain permanently from the exercise of its due influence in matters which properly concern the peace and welfare of the community of nations. Washington did not object to temporary alliances for special emergencies nor did Jefferson object to special alliances for the accomplishment of definite objects. Their advice has, however, been generally interpreted as meaning that the United States must hold aloof from world politics and attend strictly to its own business.

The Monroe Doctrine was a perfectly sound principle and it has been fully justified by nearly a century of experience. It has saved South America from the kind of exploitation to which the continents of Africa and Asia have, during the past generation, fallen a prey. The policy of isolation, on the other hand, still cherished by so many Americans as a sacred tradition of the fathers, is in principle quite distinct from the Monroe Doctrine and is in fact utterly inconsistent with the position and importance of the United States as a world power. The difference in principle between the two policies can perhaps best be illustrated by the following supposition. If the United States were to sign a permanent treaty with England placing our navy at her disposal in the event of attack from Germany or some other power, on condition that England would unite with us in opposing the intervention of any European power in Latin America, such a treaty would not be a violation of the Monroe Doctrine, but a distinct recognition of that principle. Such a treaty would, however, be a departure from our traditional policy of isolation. Of the two policies, that of avoiding political alliances is the older. It was announced by Washington under circumstances that will be considered in a moment.

In the struggle for independence the colonies deliberately sought foreign alliances. In fact, the first treaty ever signed by the United States was the treaty of alliance with France, negotiated and ratified in 1778. The aid which France extended under this treaty to our revolutionary ancestors in men, money, and ships enabled them to establish the independence of our country. A few years later came the French Revolution, the establishment of the French Republic followed by the execution of Louis XVI, and in 1793 the war between England and France. With the arrival in this country of Genet, the minister of the newly established French Republic, there began a heated debate in the newspapers throughout the country as to our obligations under the treaty of alliance and the commercial treaty of 1778. President Washington requested the opinions in writing of the members of his cabinet as to whether Genet should be received and the new government which had been set up in France recognized, as to whether the treaties were still binding, and as to whether a proclamation of neutrality should be issued. Hamilton and Jefferson replied at great length, taking as usual opposite sides, particularly on the question as to the binding force of the treaties. Hamilton took the view that as the government of Louis XVI, with which the treaties had been negotiated, had been overthrown, we were under no obligations to fulfill their stipulations and had a perfect right to renounce them. Jefferson took the correct view that the treaties were with the French nation and that they were binding under whatever government the French people chose to set up. This principle, which is now one of the fundamental doctrines of international law, was so ably expounded by Jefferson that his words are well worth quoting.

"I consider the people who constitute a society or nation as the source of all authority in that nation, as free to transact their common concerns by any agents they think proper, to change these agents individually, or the organization of them in form or function whenever they please: that all the acts done by those agents under the authority of the nation, are the acts of the nation, are obligatory on them, and enure to their use, and can in no wise be annulled or affected by any change in the form of the government, or of the persons administering it. Consequently the Treaties between the United States and France were not treaties between the United States and Louis Capet, but between the two nations of America and France, and the nations remaining in existence, tho' both of them have since changed their forms of government, the treaties are not annulled by these changes."

The argument was so heated that Washington was reluctant to press matters to a definite conclusion. From his subsequent action it appears that he agreed with Jefferson that the treaties were binding, but he held that the treaty of alliance was purely defensive and that we were under no obligation to aid France in an offensive war such as she was then waging. He accordingly issued his now famous proclamation of neutrality, April, 1793. Of this proclamation W. E. Hall, a leading English authority on international law, writing one hundred years later, said: "The policy of the United States in 1793 constitutes an epoch in the development of the usages of neutrality. There can be no doubt that it was intended and believed to give effect to the obligations then incumbent upon neutrals. But it represented by far the most advanced existing opinions as to what those obligations were; and in some points it even went farther than authoritative international custom has up to the present time advanced. In the main, however, it is identical with the standard of conduct which is now adopted by the community of nations." Washington's proclamation laid the real foundations of the American policy of isolation.

The very novelty of the rigid neutrality proclaimed by Washington made the policy a difficult one to pursue. In the Revolutionary and Napoleonic wars, which lasted for nearly a quarter of a century, the United States was the principal neutral. The problems to which this situation gave rise were so similar to the problems raised during the early years of the World War that many of the diplomatic notes prepared by Jefferson and Madison might, with a few changes of names and dates, be passed off as the correspondence of Wilson and Lansing. Washington's administration closed with the clouds of the European war still hanging heavy on the horizon. Under these circumstances he delivered his famous Farewell Address in which he said:

"The great rule of conduct for us in regard to foreign nations is, in extending our commercial relations to have with them as little *political* connection as possible. So far as we have already formed engagements let them be fulfilled with perfect good faith. Here let us stop.

"Europe has a set of primary interests which to us have none or a very remote relation. Hence she must be engaged in frequent controversies, the causes of which are essentially foreign to our concerns. Hence, therefore, it must be unwise in us to implicate ourselves by artificial ties in the ordinary vicissitudes of her politics or the ordinary combinations and collisions of her friendships or enmities.

"Our detached and distant situation invites and enables us to pursue a different course. If we remain one people, under an efficient government, the period is not far off when we may defy material injury from external annoyance; when we may take such an attitude as will cause the neutrality we may at any time resolve upon to be scrupulously respected; when belligerent nations, under the impossibility of making acquisitions upon us, will not lightly hazard the giving us provocation; when we may choose peace or war, as our interest, guided by justice, shall counsel.

"Why forego the advantages of so peculiar a situation? Why quit our own to stand upon foreign ground? Why, by interweaving our destiny with that of any part of Europe, entangle our peace and prosperity in the toils of European ambitions, rivalship, interest, humor, or caprice?

"It is our true policy to steer clear of permanent alliances with any portion of the foreign world, so far, I mean, as we are now at liberty to do it; for let me not be understood as capable of patronizing infidelity to existing engagements. I hold the maxim no less applicable to public than to private affairs that honesty is always the best policy. I repeat, therefore, let those engagements be observed in their genuine sense. But in my opinion it is unnecessary and would be unwise to extend them.

"Taking care always to keep ourselves by suitable establishments on a respectable defensive posture, we may safely trust to temporary alliances for extraordinary emergencies."

It will be observed that Washington warned his countrymen against *permanent* alliances. He expressly said that we might "safely trust to *temporary* alliances for extraordinary emergencies." Further than this many of those who are continually quoting Washington's warning against alliances not only fail to note the limitations under which the advice was given, but they also overlook the reasons assigned. In a succeeding paragraph of the Farewell Address he said:

"With me a predominant motive has been to endeavor to gain time to our country to settle and mature its yet recent institutions, and to progress without interruption to that degree of strength and consistency which is necessary to give it, humanly speaking, the command of its own fortunes."

The expression "entangling alliances" does not occur in the Farewell Address, but was given currency by Jefferson. In his first inaugural address he summed up the principles by which he proposed to regulate his foreign policy in the following terms: "Peace, commerce, and honest friendship with all nations, entangling alliances with none."

During the brief interval of peace following the treaty of Amiens in 1801, Napoleon undertook the reëstablishment of French power in Santo Domingo as the first step in the development of a colonial empire which he determined upon when he forced Spain to retrocede Louisiana to France by the secret treaty of San Ildefonso in 1800. Fortunately for us the ill-fated expedition to Santo Domingo encountered the opposition of half a million negroes and ultimately fell a prey to the ravages of yellow fever. As soon as Jefferson heard of the cession of Louisiana to France, he instructed Livingston, his representative at Paris, to open negotiations for the purchase of New Orleans and West Florida, stating that the acquisition of New Orleans by a powerful nation like France would inevitably lead to friction and conflict. "The day that France takes possession of New Orleans fixes the sentence which is to restrain her forever within her low water mark. It seals the union of two nations who in conjunction can maintain exclusive possession of the ocean. From that moment we must marry ourselves to the British fleet and nation. We must turn all our attentions to a maritime force, for which our resources place us on very high grounds: and having formed and cemented together a power which may render reinforcement of her settlements here impossible to France, make the first cannon, which shall be fired in Europe the signal for tearing up any settlement she may have made, and for holding the two continents of America in sequestration for the common purposes of the united British and American nations. This is not a state of things we seek or desire. It is one which this measure, if adopted by France, forces on us, as necessarily as any other cause, by the laws of nature, brings on its necessary effect."

Monroe was later sent to Paris to support Livingston and he was instructed, in case there was no prospect of a favorable termination of the negotiations, to avoid a rupture until the spring and "in the meantime enter into conferences with the British Government, through their ambassador at Paris, to fix principles of alliance, and leave us in peace until Congress meets." Jefferson had already informed the British minister at Washington that if France should, by closing the mouth of the Mississippi, force the United States to war, "they would throw away the scabbard." Monroe and Livingston were now instructed, in case they should become convinced that France meditated hostilities against the United States, to negotiate an alliance with England and to stipulate that neither party should make peace or truce without the consent of the other. Thus notwithstanding his French proclivities and his warning against "entangling alliances," the author of the immortal Declaration of Independence was ready and willing in this emergency to form an alliance with England. The unexpected cession of the entire province of Louisiana to the United States made the contemplated alliance with England unnecessary.

The United States was no more successful in its effort to remain neutral during the Napoleonic wars than it was during the late war, though the slow means of communication a hundred years ago caused the struggle for neutral rights to be drawn out for a much longer period of time. Neither England nor France regarded us as having any rights which they were bound to respect, and American commerce was fairly bombarded by French decrees and British orders in council. There was really not much more reason why we should have fought England than France, but as England's naval supremacy enabled her to interfere more effectually with our commerce on the sea and as this interference was accompanied by the practice of impressing American sailors into the British service, we finally declared war against her. No effort was made, however, to form an alliance or even to coöperate with Napoleon. The United States fought the War of

1812 without allies, and while we gained a number of single-ship actions and notable victories on Lake Erie and Lake Champlain, we failed utterly in two campaigns to occupy Canada, and the final result of the conflict was that our national capitol was burned and our commerce absolutely swept from the seas. Jackson's victory at New Orleans, while gratifying to our pride, took place two weeks after the treaty of Ghent had been signed and had, consequently, no effect on the outcome of the war.

II

FORMULATION OF THE MONROE DOCTRINE

The international situation which gave rise to the Monroe Doctrine was the most unusual in some respects that modern history records. The European alliance which had been organized in 1813 for the purpose of bringing about the overthrow of Napoleon continued to dominate the affairs of Europe until 1823. This alliance, which met at the Congress of Vienna in 1815 and held later meetings at Aix-la-Chapelle in 1818, at Troppau in 1820, at Laybach in 1821, and at Verona in 1822, undertook to legislate for all Europe and was the nearest approach to a world government that had ever been tried. While this alliance publicly proclaimed that it had no other object than the maintenance of peace and that the repose of the world was its motive and its end, its real object was to uphold absolute monarchy and to suppress every attempt at the establishment of representative government. As long as England remained in the alliance her statesmen exercised a restraining influence, for England was the only one of the allies which professed to have a representative system of government. As Castlereagh was setting out for the meeting at Aix-la-Chapelle Lord Liverpool, who was then prime minister, warned him that, "The Russian must be made to feel that we have a parliament and a public, to which we are responsible, and that we cannot permit ourselves to be drawn into views of policy which are wholly incompatible with the spirit of our government."

The reactionary spirit of the continental members of the alliance was soon thoroughly aroused by the series of revolutions that followed one another in 1820. In March the Spanish army turned against the government of Ferdinand VII and demanded the restoration of the constitution of 1812. The action of the army was everywhere approved and sustained by the people and the king was forced to proclaim the constitution and to promise to uphold it. The Spanish revolution was followed in July by a constitutional movement in Naples, and in August by a similar movement in Portugal; while the next year witnessed the outbreak of the Greek struggle for independence. Thus in all three of the peninsulas of Southern Europe the people were struggling for the right of self-government. The great powers at once took alarm at the rapid spread of revolutionary ideas and proceeded to adopt measures for the suppression of the movements to which these ideas gave rise. At Troppau and Laybach measures were taken for the suppression of the revolutionary movements in Italy. An Austrian army entered Naples in March, 1821, overthrew the constitutional government that had been inaugurated, and restored Ferdinand II to absolute power. The revolution which had broken out in Piedmont was also suppressed by a detachment of the Austrian army. England held aloof from all participation in the conferences at Troppau and Laybach, though her ambassador to Austria was present to watch the proceedings.

The next meeting of the allied powers was arranged for October, 1822, at Verona. Here the affairs of Greece, Italy, and in particular Spain came up for consideration. At this congress all five powers of the alliance were represented. France was especially concerned about the condition of affairs in Spain, and England sent Wellington out of self-defense. The Congress of Verona was devoted largely to a discussion of Spanish affairs. Wellington had been instructed to use all his influence against the adoption of measures of intervention in Spain. When he found that the other powers were bent upon this step and that his protest would be unheeded, he withdrew from the congress. The four remaining powers signed the secret treaty of Verona, November 22, 1822, as a revision, so they declared in the preamble, of the Treaty of the Holy Alliance, which had been signed at Paris in 1815 by Austria, Russia, and Prussia. This last mentioned treaty sprang from the erratic brain of the Czar Alexander under the influence of Baroness Krüdener, and is one of the most remarkable political documents extant. No one had taken it seriously except the Czar himself and it had been without influence upon the politics of Europe. The text of the treaty of Verona was never officially published, but the following articles soon appeared in the press of Europe and America:

"Article I.—The high contracting powers being convinced that the system of representative government is equally as incompatible with the monarchical principles as the maxim of the sovereignty of the people with the divine right, engage mutually, in the most solemn manner, to use all their efforts to put an end to the system of representative governments, in whatever country it may exist in Europe, and to prevent its being introduced in those countries where it is not yet known.

"Article II.—As it cannot be doubted that the liberty of the press is the most powerful means used by the pretended supporters of the rights of nations, to the detriment of those of Princes, the high contracting parties promise reciprocally to adopt all proper measures to suppress it, not only in their own states, but, also, in the rest of Europe.

"Article III.—Convinced that the principles of religion contribute most powerfully to keep nations in the state of passive obedience which they owe to their Princes, the high contracting parties declare it to be their intention to sustain, in their respective states, those measures which the clergy may adopt, with the aim of ameliorating their own interests, so intimately connected with the preservation of the authority of Princes; and the contracting powers join in offering their thanks to the Pope, for what he has already done for them, and solicit his constant coöperation in their views of submitting the nations.

"Article IV.—The situation of Spain and Portugal unite unhappily all the circumstances to which this treaty has particular reference. The high contracting parties, in confiding to France the care of putting an end to them, engage to assist her in the manner which may the least compromise them with their own people and the people of France, by means of a subsidy on the part of the two empires, of twenty millions of francs every year, from the date of the signature of this treaty to the end of the war."

Such was the code of despotism which the continental powers adopted for Europe and which they later proposed to extend to America. It was an attempt to make the world safe for autocracy. Wellington's protest at Verona marked the final withdrawal of England from the alliance which had overthrown Napoleon and naturally inclined her toward a rapprochement with the United States. The aim of the Holy Allies, as the remaining members of the alliance now called themselves, was to undo the work of the Revolution and of Napoleon and to restore all the peoples of Europe to the absolute sway of their legitimate sovereigns. After the overthrow of the constitutional movements in Piedmont, Naples, and Spain, absolutism reigned supreme once more in western Europe, but the Holy Allies felt that their task was not completed so long as Spain's revolted colonies in America remained unsubjugated. These colonies had drifted into practical independence while Napoleon's brother Joseph was on the throne of Spain. Nelson's great victory at Trafalgar had left England supreme on the seas and neither Napoleon nor Joseph had been able to establish any control over Spain's American colonies. When Ferdinand was restored to his throne in 1814, he unwisely undertook to refasten on his colonies the yoke of the old colonial system and to break up the commerce which had grown up with

England and with the United States. The different colonies soon proclaimed their independence and the wars of liberation ensued. By 1822 it was evident that Spain unassisted could never resubjugate them, and the United States after mature deliberation recognized the new republics and established diplomatic intercourse with them. England, although enjoying the full benefits of trade with the late colonies of Spain, still hesitated out of regard for the mother country to take the final step of recognition.

In the late summer of 1823 circular letters were issued inviting the powers to a conference at Paris to consider the Spanish-American question. George Canning, the British foreign secretary, at once called into conference Richard Rush, the American minister, and proposed joint action against the schemes of the Holy Alliance. Rush replied that he was not authorized to enter into such an agreement, but that he would communicate the proposal at once to his government. As soon as Rush's dispatch was received President Monroe realized fully the magnitude of the issue presented by the proposal of an Anglo-American alliance. Before submitting the matter to his cabinet he transmitted copies of Rush's dispatch to ex-Presidents Jefferson and Madison and the following interesting correspondence took place. In his letter to Jefferson of October 17th, the President said:

"I transmit to you two despatches, which were receiv'd from Mr. Rush, while I was lately in Washington, which involve interests of the highest importance. They contain two letters from Mr. Canning, suggesting designs of the holy alliance, against the Independence of So. America, & proposing a co-operation, between G. Britain & the U States, in support of it, against the members of that alliance. The project aims, in the first instance, at a mere expression of opinion, somewhat in the abstract, but which, it is expected by Mr. Canning, will have a great political effect, by defeating the combination. By Mr. Rush's answers, which are also enclosed, you will see the light in which he views the subject, & the extent to which he may have gone. Many important considerations are involved in this proposition. 1st Shall we entangle ourselves, at all, in European politicks, & wars, on the side of any power, against others, presuming that a concert, by agreement, of the kind proposed, may lead to that result? 2d If a case can exist in which a sound maxim may, & ought to be departed from, is not the present instance, precisely that case? 3d Has not the epoch arriv'd when G. Britain must take her stand, either on the side of the monarchs of Europe, or of the U States, & in consequence, either in favor of Despotism or of liberty & may it not be presum'd that, aware of that necessity, her government has seiz'd on the present occurrence, as that, which it deems, the most suitable, to announce & mark the commenc'ment of that career?

"My own impression is that we ought to meet the proposal of the British govt. & to make it known, that we would view an interference on the part of the European powers, and especially an attack on the Colonies, by them, as an attack on ourselves, presuming that, if they succeeded with them, they would extend it to us. I am sensible however of the extent & difficulty of the question, & shall be happy to have yours, & Mr. Madison's opinions on it."

Jefferson's reply dated Monticello, October 24th, displays not only a profound insight into the international situation, but a wide vision of the possibilities involved. He said:

"The question presented by the letters you have sent me, is the most momentous which has ever been offered to my contemplation since that of Independence. That made us a nation, this sets our compass and points the course which we are to steer through the ocean of time opening on us. And never could we embark on it under circumstances more auspicious. Our first and fundamental maxim should be, never to entangle ourselves in the broils of Europe. Our second, never to suffer Europe to intermeddle with cis-Atlantic affairs. America, North and South, has a set of interests distinct from those of Europe, and peculiarly her own. She should therefore have a system of her own, separate and apart from that of Europe. While the last is laboring to become the domicil of despotism, our endeavor should surely be, to make our hemisphere that of freedom. One nation, most of all, could disturb us in this pursuit; she now offers to lead, aid, and accompany us in it. By acceding to her proposition, we detach her from the bands, bring her mighty weight into the scale of free government, and emancipate a continent at one stroke, which might otherwise linger long in doubt and difficulty. Great Britain is the nation which can do us the most harm of any one, or all on earth; and with her on our side we need not fear the whole world. With her then, we should most sedulously cherish a cordial friendship; and nothing would tend more to knit our affections than to be fighting once more, side by side, in the same cause. Not that I would purchase even her amity at the price of taking part in her wars. But the war in which the present proposition might engage us, should that be its consequence, is not her war, but ours. Its object is to introduce and establish the American system, of keeping out of our land all foreign powers, of never permitting those of Europe to intermeddle with the affairs of our nations. It is to maintain our own principle, not to depart from it. And if, to facilitate this, we can effect a division in the body of the European powers, and draw over to our side its most powerful member, surely we should do it. But I am clearly of Mr. Canning's opinion, that it will prevent instead of provoking war. With Great Britain withdrawn from their scale and shifted into that of our two continents, all Europe combined would not undertake such a war. For how would they propose to get at either enemy without superior fleets? Nor is the occasion to be slighted which this proposition offers, of declaring our protest against the atrocious violations of the rights of nations, by the interference of any one in the internal affairs of another, so flagitiously begun by Bonaparte, and now continued by the equally lawless Alliance, calling itself Holy."

Madison not only agreed with Jefferson as to the wisdom of accepting the British proposal of some form of joint action, but he went even further and suggested that the declaration should not be limited to the American republics, but that it should express disapproval of the late invasion of Spain and of any interference with the Greeks who were then struggling for independence from Turkey. Monroe, it appears, was strongly inclined to act on Madison's suggestion, but his cabinet took a different view of the situation. From the diary of John Quincy Adams, Monroe's secretary of state, it appears that almost the whole of November was taken up by cabinet discussions on Canning's proposals and on Russia's aggressions in the northwest. Adams stoutly opposed any alliance or joint declaration with Great Britain. The composition of the President's message remained in doubt until the 27th, when the more conservative views of Adams were, according to his own statement of the case, adopted. He advocated an independent course of action on the part of the United States, without direct reference to Canning's proposals, though substantially in accord with them. Adams defined his position as follows: "The ground that I wish to take is that of earnest remonstrance against the interference of the European powers by force with South America, but to disclaim all interference on our part with Europe; to make an American cause and adhere inflexibly to that." Adams's dissent from Monroe's position was, it is claimed, due partly to the influence of Clay who advocated a Pan-American system, partly to the fact that the proposed coöperation with Great Britain would bind the United States not to acquire some of the coveted parts of the Spanish possessions, and partly to the fear that the United States as the ally of Great Britain would be compelled to play a secondary part. He probably carried his point by showing that the same ends could be accomplished by an independent declaration, since it was evident that the sea power of Great Britain would be used to prevent the reconquest of South America by the European powers. Monroe, as we have seen, thought that the exigencies of the situation justified a departure from the sound maxim of political isolation, and in this opinion he was supported by his two predecessors in the presidency.

The opinions of Monroe, Jefferson, and Madison in favor of an alliance with Great Britain and a broad declaration against the intervention of the great powers in the affairs of weaker states in any part of the world, have been severely criticised by some historians and ridiculed by others, but time and circumstances often bring about a complete change in our point of view. After the beginning of the great world conflict, especially after our entrance into it, several writers raised the question as to whether, after all, the three elder statesmen were not right and Adams and Clay wrong. If the United States and England had come out in favor of a general declaration against intervention in the concerns of small states and established it as a world-wide principle, the course of human history during the next century might have been very different, but Adams's diary does not tell the whole story. On his own statement of the case he might be justly censured by posterity for persuading the president to take a narrow American view of a question which was world-wide in its bearing. An important element in the situation, however, was Canning's change of attitude between the time of his conference with Rush in August and the formulation of the president's message. Two days after the delivery of his now famous message Monroe wrote to Jefferson in explanation of the form the declaration had taken: "Mr. Canning's zeal has much abated of late." It appears from Rush's correspondence that the only thing which stood in the way of joint action by the two powers was Canning's unwillingness to extend immediate recognition to the South American republics. On August 27th, Rush stated to Canning that it would greatly facilitate joint action if England would acknowledge at once the full independence of the South American colonies.

In communicating the account of this interview to his government Mr. Rush concluded: "Should I be asked by Mr. Canning, whether, in case the recognition be made by Great Britain without more delay, I am on my part prepared to make a declaration, in the name of my government, that it will not remain inactive under an attack upon the independence of those states by the Holy Alliance, the present determination of my judgment is that I will make such a declaration explicitly, and avow it before the world." About three weeks later Canning, who was growing restless at the delay in hearing from Washington, again urged Rush to act without waiting for specific instructions from his government. He tried to show that the proposed joint declaration would not conflict with the American policy of avoiding entangling alliances, for the question at issue was American as much as European, if not more. Rush then indicated his willingness to act provided England would "immediately and unequivocally acknowledge the independence of the new states." Canning did not care to extend full recognition to the South American states until he could do so without giving unnecessary offense to Spain and the allies, and he asked if Mr. Rush could not give his assent to the proposal on a promise of future recognition. Mr. Rush refused to accede to anything but immediate acknowledgment of independence and so the matter ended.

As Canning could not come to a formal understanding with the United States, he determined to make a frank avowal of the views of the British cabinet to France and to this end he had an interview with Prince Polignac, the French ambassador at London, October 9, 1823, in which he declared that Great Britain had no desire to hasten recognition, but that any foreign interference, by force, or by menace, would be a motive for immediate recognition; that England "could not go into a joint deliberation upon the subject of Spanish America upon an equal footing with other powers, whose opinions were less formed upon that question." This declaration drew from Polignac the admission that he considered the reduction of the colonies by Spain as hopeless and that France "abjured in any case, any design of acting against the colonies by force of arms." This admission was a distinct victory for Canning, in that it prepared the way for ultimate recognition by England, and an account of the interview was communicated without delay to the allied courts. The interview was not communicated to Rush until the latter part of November, and therefore had no influence upon the formation of Monroe's message.

The Monroe Doctrine is comprised in two widely separated paragraphs that occur in the message of December 2, 1823. The first, relating to Russia's encroachments on the northwest coast, and occurring near the beginning of the message, was an assertion to the effect that the American continents had assumed an independent condition and were no longer open to European colonization. This may be regarded as a statement of fact. No part of the continent at that time remained unclaimed. The second paragraph, relating to Spanish America and occurring near the close of the message, was a declaration against the extension to the American continents of the system of intervention adopted by the Holy Alliance for the suppression of popular government in Europe.

The language used by President Monroe is as follows:

1. "At the proposal of the Russian Imperial Government, made through the minister of the Emperor residing here, a full power and instructions have been transmitted to the minister of the United States at St. Petersburg to arrange by amicable negotiation the respective rights and interests of the two nations on the north-west coast of this continent. A similar proposal had been made by His Imperial Majesty to the Government of Great Britain, which has likewise been acceded to. The Government of the United States has been desirous by this friendly proceeding of manifesting the great value which they have invariably attached to the friendship of the Emperor

and their solicitude to cultivate the best understanding with his Government. In the discussions to which this interest has given rise and in the arrangements by which they may terminate the occasion has been judged proper for asserting, as a principle in which the rights and interests of the United States are involved, that the American continents, by the free and independent condition which they have assumed and maintain, are henceforth not to be considered as subjects for future colonization by any European powers."

2. "In the wars of the European powers in matters relating to themselves we have never taken any part, nor does it comport with our policy so to do. It is only when our rights are invaded or seriously menaced that we resent injuries or make preparation for our defense. With the movements in this hemisphere we are of necessity more immediately connected, and by causes which must be obvious to all enlightened and impartial observers. The political system of the allied powers is essentially different in this respect from that of America. This difference proceeds from that which exists in their respective Governments; and to the defense of our own, which has been achieved by the loss of so much blood and treasure, and matured by the wisdom of their most enlightened citizens, and under which we have enjoyed unexampled felicity, this whole nation is devoted. We owe it, therefore, to candor and to the amicable relations existing between the United States and those powers to declare that we should consider any attempt on their part to extend their system to any portion of this hemisphere as dangerous to our peace and safety. With the existing colonies or dependencies of any European power we have not interfered and shall not interfere. But with the Governments who have declared their independence and maintained it, and whose independence we have, on great consideration and on just principles, acknowledged, we could not view any interposition for the purpose of oppressing them, or controlling in any other

manner their destiny, by any European power in any other light than as the manifestation of an unfriendly disposition toward the United States."

The message made a profound impression on the world, all the more profound for the fact that Canning's interview with Polignac was known only to the chancelleries of Europe. To the public at large it appeared that the United States was blazing the way for democracy and liberty and that Canning was holding back through fear of giving offense to the allies. The governments of Europe realized only too well that Monroe's declaration would be backed by the British navy, and all thought of intervention in Latin America was therefore abandoned. A few months later England formally recognized the independence of the Spanish-American republics, and Canning made his famous boast on the floor of the House of Commons. In a speech delivered December 12, 1826, in defense of his position in not having arrested the French invasion of Spain, he said: "I looked another way—I sought for compensation in another hemisphere. Contemplating Spain, such as our ancestors had known her, I resolved that, if France had Spain, it should not be Spain *with the Indies*. I called the New World into existence to redress the balance of the Old."

III

THE MONROE DOCTRINE AND THE EUROPEAN BALANCE OF POWER

President Monroe said in effect that the western hemisphere must be made safe for democracy. It was reserved for our own generation and for President Wilson to extend the declaration and to say that the world must be made safe for democracy. President Monroe announced that we would uphold international law and republican government in this hemisphere, and as *quid pro quo* he announced that it was the settled policy of the United States to refrain from all interference in the internal affairs of European states. He based his declaration, therefore, not mainly on right and justice, but on the doctrine of the separation of the European and American spheres of politics. The Monroe Doctrine and the policy of isolation thus became linked together in the public mind as compensating policies, neither one of which could stand without the other. Even Secretary Olney as late as 1895 declared that "American non-intervention in Europe implied European non-intervention in America." It is not strange, therefore, that the public at large should regard the policy of isolation as the sole justification for the Monroe Doctrine. There is, however, neither logic nor justice in basing our right to uphold law and freedom in this hemisphere on our promise not to interfere with the violation of law and humanity in Europe. The real difficulty is that the Monroe Doctrine as interpreted in recent years has developed certain imperialistic tendencies and that the imperialistic implications of the policy resemble too closely the imperialistic aims of the European powers.

For three quarters of a century after Monroe's declaration the policy of isolation was more rigidly adhered to than ever, the principal departure from it being the signature and ratification of the Clayton-Bulwer Treaty in 1850. By the terms of this treaty we recognized a joint British interest in any canal that might be built through the isthmus connecting North and South America, undertook to establish the general neutralization of such canal, and agreed to invite other powers, European and American, to unite in protecting the same. Owing to differences that soon arose between the United States and England as to the interpretation of the treaty, the clause providing for the adherence of other powers was never carried out.

For nearly a hundred years we have successfully upheld the Monroe Doctrine without a resort to force. The policy has never been favorably regarded by the powers of continental Europe. Bismarck described it as "an international impertinence." In recent years it has stirred up rather intense opposition in certain parts of Latin America. Until recently no American writers appear to have considered the real nature of the sanction on which the doctrine rested. How is it that without an army and until recent years without a navy of any size we have been able to uphold a policy which has been described as an impertinence to Latin America and a standing defiance to Europe? Americans generally seem to think that the Monroe Doctrine has in it an inherent sanctity which prevents other nations from violating it. In view of the general disregard of sanctities, inherent or acquired, during the early stages of the late war, this explanation will not hold good and some other must be sought. Americans have been so little concerned with international affairs that they have failed to see any connection between the Monroe Doctrine and the balance of power in Europe. The existence of a European balance of power is the only explanation of our having been able to uphold the Monroe Doctrine for so long a time without a resort to force. Some one or more of the European powers would long ago have stepped in and called our bluff, that is, forced us to repudiate the Monroe Doctrine or fight for it, had it not been for the well-grounded fear that as soon as they became engaged with us some other European power would attack them in the rear. A few illustrations will be sufficient to establish this thesis.

The most serious strain to which the Monroe Doctrine was ever subjected was the attempt of Louis Napoleon during the American Civil War to establish the empire of Maximilian in Mexico under French auspices. He was clever enough to induce England and Spain to go in with him in 1861 for the avowed purpose of collecting the claims of their subjects against the government of Mexico. Before the joint intervention had gone very far, however, these two powers became convinced that Napoleon had ulterior designs and withdrew their forces. Napoleon's Mexican venture was deliberately calculated on the success of the Southern Confederacy. Hence, his friendly relations with the Confederate commissioners and the talk of an alliance between the Confederacy and Maximilian backed by the power of France. Against each successive step taken by France in Mexico Mr. Seward, Lincoln's Secretary of State, protested. As the Civil War drew to a successful conclusion his protests became more and more emphatic. Finally, in the spring of 1866, the United States Government began massing troops on the Mexican border and Mr. Seward sent what was practically an ultimatum to the French Emperor; he requested to know when the long-promised withdrawal of the French troops would take place. Napoleon replied, fixing the dates for their withdrawal in three separate detachments.

American historians have usually attributed Napoleon's backdown to Seward's diplomacy supported by the military power of the United States, which was, of course, greater then than at any previous time in our history. All this undoubtedly had its effect on Napoleon's mind, but it appears that conditions in Europe just at that particular moment had an even greater influence in causing him to abandon his Mexican scheme. Within a few days of the receipt of Seward's ultimatum Napoleon was informed of

Bismarck's determination to force a war with Austria over the Schleswig-Holstein controversy. Napoleon realized that the territorial aggrandizement of Prussia, without any corresponding gains by France, would be a serious blow to his prestige and in fact endanger his throne. He at once entered upon a long and hazardous diplomatic game in which Bismarck outplayed him and eventually forced him into war. In order to have a free hand to meet the European situation he decided to yield to the American demands. As the European situation developed he hastened the final withdrawal of his troops and left Maximilian to his fate. Thus the Monroe Doctrine was vindicated!

Let us take next President Cleveland's intervention in the Venezuelan boundary dispute. Here surely was a clear and spectacular vindication of the Monroe Doctrine which no one can discount. Let us briefly examine the facts. Some 30,000 square miles of territory on the border of Venezuela and British Guiana were in dispute. Venezuela, a weak and helpless state, had offered to submit the question to arbitration. Great Britain, powerful and overbearing, refused. After Secretary Olney, in a long correspondence ably conducted, had failed to move the British Government, President Cleveland decided to intervene. In a message to Congress in December, 1895, he reviewed the controversy at length, declared that the acquisition of territory in America by a European power through the arbitrary advance of a boundary line was a clear violation of the Monroe Doctrine, and asked Congress for an appropriation to pay the expenses of a commission which he proposed to appoint for the purpose of determining the true boundary, which he said it would then be our duty to uphold. Lest there should be any misunderstanding as to his intentions he solemnly added: "In making these recommendations I am fully alive to the responsibility incurred and keenly realize all the consequences that may follow." Congress promptly voted the appropriation.

Here was a bold and unqualified defiance of England. No one before had ever trod so roughly on the British lion's tail with impunity. The English-speaking public on both sides of the Atlantic was stunned and amazed. Outside of diplomatic circles few persons were aware that any subject of controversy between the two countries existed, and no one had any idea that it was of a serious nature. Suddenly the two nations found themselves on the point of war. After the first outburst of indignation the storm passed; and before the American boundary commission completed its investigation England signed an arbitration agreement with Venezuela. Some persons, after looking in vain for an explanation, have concluded that Lord Salisbury's failure to deal more seriously with Mr. Cleveland's affront to the British Government was due to his sense of humor.

But here again the true explanation is to be found in events that were happening in another quarter of the globe. Cleveland's Venezuelan message was sent to Congress on December 17th. At the end of the year came Dr. Jameson's raid into the Transvaal and on the third of January the German Kaiser sent his famous telegram of congratulation to Paul Kruger. The wrath of England was suddenly diverted from America to Germany, and Lord Salisbury avoided a rupture with the United States over a matter which after all was not of such serious moment to England in order to be free to deal with a question involving much greater interests in South Africa. The Monroe Doctrine was none the less effectively vindicated.

In 1902 Germany made a carefully planned and determined effort to test out the Monroe Doctrine and see whether we would fight for it. In that year Germany, England, and Italy made a naval demonstration against Venezuela for the purpose of forcing her to recognize as valid certain claims of their subjects. How England was led into the trap is still a mystery, but the Kaiser thought that he had her thoroughly committed, that if England once started in with him she could not turn against him. But he had evidently not profited by the experience of Napoleon III in Mexico. Through the mediation of Herbert Bowen, the American minister, Venezuela agreed to recognize in principle the claims of the foreign powers and to arbitrate the amount. England and Italy accepted this offer and withdrew their squadrons. Germany, however, remained for a time obdurate. This much was known at the time.

A rather sensational account of what followed next has recently been made public in Thayer's "Life and Letters of John Hay." Into the merits of the controversy that arose over Thayer's version of the Roosevelt-Holleben interview it is not necessary to enter. The significant fact, that Germany withdrew from Venezuela under pressure, is, however, amply established. Admiral Dewey stated publicly that the entire American fleet was assembled at the time under his command in Porto Rican waters ready to move at a moment's notice. Why did Germany back down from her position? Her navy was supposed to be at least as powerful as ours. The reason why the Kaiser concluded not to measure strength with the United States was that England had accepted arbitration and withdrawn her support and he did not dare attack the United States with the British navy in his rear. Again the nicely adjusted European balance prevented the Monroe Doctrine from being put to the test of actual war.

While England has from time to time objected to some of the corollaries deduced from the Monroe Doctrine, she has on the whole been not unfavorably disposed toward the essential features of that policy. The reason for this is that the Monroe Doctrine has been an open-door policy, and has thus been in general accord with the British policy of free trade. The United States has not used the Monroe Doctrine for the establishment of exclusive trade relations with our southern neighbors. In fact, we have largely neglected the South American countries as a field for the development of American commerce. The failure to cultivate this field has not been due wholly to neglect, however, but to the fact that we have had employment for all our capital at home and consequently have not been in a position to aid in the industrial development of the Latin-American states, and to the further fact that our exports have been so largely the same and hence the trade of both North and South America has been mainly with Europe. There has, therefore, been little rivalry between the United States and the powers of Europe in the field of South American commerce. Our interest has been political rather than commercial. We have prevented the establishment of spheres of influence and preserved the open door. This situation has been in full accord with British policy. Had Great Britain adopted a high tariff policy and been compelled to demand commercial concessions from Latin America by force, the Monroe Doctrine would long since have gone by the board and been forgotten. Americans should not forget the fact, moreover, that at any time during the past twenty years Great Britain could have settled all her outstanding difficulties with Germany by agreeing to sacrifice the Monroe Doctrine and give her rival a free hand in South America. In the face of such a combination our navy would have been of little avail.

IV

INTERNATIONAL COOPERATION WITHOUT THE SANCTION OF FORCE

President Monroe's declaration had a negative as well as a positive side. It was in effect an announcement to the world that we would not use force in support of law and justice anywhere except in the Western Hemisphere, that we intended to stay at home and mind our own business. Washington and Jefferson had recommended a policy of isolation on grounds of expediency. Washington, as we have seen, regarded this policy as a temporary expedient, while Jefferson upon two separate occasions was ready to form an alliance with England. Probably neither one of them contemplated the possibility of the United States shirking its responsibilities as a member of the family of nations. Monroe's message contained the implied promise that if Europe would refrain from interfering in the political concerns of this hemisphere, we would abstain from all intervention in Europe. From that day until our entrance into the World War it was generally understood, and on numerous occasions officially proclaimed, that the United States would not resort to force on any question arising outside of America except where its material interests were directly involved. We have not refrained from diplomatic action in matters not strictly American, but it has always been understood that such action would not be backed by force. In the existing state of world politics this limitation has been a serious handicap to American diplomacy. To take what we could get and to give nothing in return has been a hard rule for our diplomats, and has greatly circumscribed their activities. Diplomatic action without the use or threat of force has, however, accomplished something in the world at large, so that American influence has by no means been limited to the western hemisphere.

During the first half of the nineteenth century the subject of slavery absorbed a large part of the attention of American statesmen. The fact that they were not concerned with foreign problems outside of the American hemisphere probably caused them to devote more time and attention to this subject than they would otherwise have done. Slavery and isolation had a very narrowing effect on men in public life, especially during the period from 1830 to 1860. As the movement against slavery in the early thirties became world-wide, the retention of the "peculiar institution" in this country had the effect of increasing our isolation. The effort of the American Colonization Society to solve or mitigate the problem of slavery came very near giving us a colony in Africa. In fact, Liberia, the negro republic founded on the west coast of Africa by the Colonization Society, was in all essentials an American protectorate, though the United States carefully refrained in its communications with other powers from doing more than expressing its good will for the little republic. As Liberia was founded years before Africa became a field for European exploitation, it was suffered to pursue its course without outside interference, and the United States was never called upon to decide whether its diplomatic protection would be backed up by force.

The slave trade was a subject of frequent discussion between the United States and England during the first half of the nineteenth century, and an arrangement for its suppression was finally embodied in Article VIII of the Webster-Ashburton Treaty of 1842. The only reason why the two countries had never been able to act in accord on this question before was that Great Britain persistently refused to renounce the right of impressment which she had exercised in the years preceding the War of 1812. The United States therefore refused to sign any agreement which would permit British naval officers to search American vessels in time of peace. In 1820 the United States declared the slave trade to be a form of piracy, and Great Britain advanced the view that as there was no doubt of the right of a naval officer to visit and search a ship suspected of piracy, her officers should be permitted to visit and search ships found off the west coast of Africa under the American flag which were suspected of being engaged in the slave trade. The United States stoutly refused to acquiesce in this view. In the Webster-Ashburton Treaty of 1842 it was finally agreed that each of the two powers should maintain on the coast of Africa a sufficient squadron "to enforce, separately and respectively, the laws, rights, and obligations of each of the two countries for the suppression of the slave trade." It was further agreed that the officers should act in concert and coöperation, but the agreement was so worded as to avoid all possibility of our being drawn into an entangling alliance.

The United States has upon various occasions expressed a humanitarian interest in the natives of Africa. In 1884 two delegates were sent to the Berlin conference which adopted a general act giving a recognized status to the Kongo Free State. The American delegates signed the treaty in common with the delegates of the European powers, but it was not submitted to the Senate for ratification for reasons stated as follows by President Cleveland in his annual message of December 8, 1885:

"A conference of delegates of the principal commercial nations was held at Berlin last winter to discuss methods whereby the Kongo basin might be kept open to the world's trade. Delegates attended on behalf of the United States on the understanding that their part should be merely deliberative, without imparting to the results any binding character so far as the United States were concerned. This reserve was due to the indisposition of this

Government to share in any disposal by an international congress of jurisdictional questions in remote foreign territories. The results of the conference were embodied in a formal act of the nature of an international convention, which laid down certain obligations purporting to be binding on the signatories, subject to ratification within one year. Notwithstanding the reservation under which the delegates of the United States attended, their signatures were attached to the general act in the same manner as those of the plenipotentiaries of other governments, thus making the United States appear, without reserve or qualification, as signatories to a joint international engagement imposing on the signers the conservation of the territorial integrity of distant regions where we have no established interests or control.

"This Government does not, however, regard its reservation of liberty of action in the premises as at all impaired; and holding that an engagement to share in the obligation of enforcing neutrality in the remote valley of the Kongo would be an alliance whose responsibilities we are not in a position to assume, I abstain from asking the sanction of the Senate to that general act."

The United States also sent delegates to the international conference held at Brussels in 1890 for the purpose of dealing with the slave trade in certain unappropriated regions of Central Africa. The American delegates insisted that prohibitive duties should be imposed on the importation of spirituous liquors into the Kongo. The European representatives, being unwilling to incorporate the American proposals, framed a separate tariff convention for the Kongo, which the American delegates refused to sign. The latter did, however, affix their signatures to the general treaty which provided for the suppression of the African slave trade and the restriction of the sale of firearms, ammunition, and spirituous liquors in certain parts of the African continent. In ratifying the treaty the Senate reaffirmed the American policy of isolation in the following resolution:

"That the United States of America, having neither possessions nor protectorates in Africa, hereby disclaims any intention, in ratifying this treaty, to indicate any interest whatsoever in the possessions or protectorates established or claimed on that Continent by the other powers, or any approval of the wisdom, expediency or lawfulness thereof, and does not join in any expressions in the said General Act which might be construed as such a declaration or acknowledgement; and, for this reason, that it is desirable that a copy of this resolution be inserted in the protocol to be drawn up at the time of the exchange of the ratifications of this treaty on the part of the United States."

The United States has always stood for legality in international relations and has always endeavored to promote the arbitration of international disputes. Along these lines we have achieved notable success. It is, of course, sometimes difficult to separate questions of international law from questions of international politics. We have been so scrupulous in our efforts to keep out of political entanglements that we have sometimes failed to uphold principles of law in the validity of which we were as much concerned as any other nation. We have always recognized international law as a part of the law of the land, and we have always acknowledged the moral responsibilities that rested on us as a member of the society of nations. In fact, the Constitution of the United States expressly recognizes the binding force of the law of nations and of treaties. As international law is the only law that governs the relations between states, we are, of course, directly concerned in the enforcement of existing law and in the development of new law. When the Declaration of Paris was drawn up by

Most of the conventions adopted by the second Hague Conference were ratified by the United States without reservation. The fact, however, that certain of these conventions were not ratified by all the powers represented at the Conference, and that others were ratified with important reservations, left the status of most of the conventions in doubt, so that at the beginning of the World War there was great confusion as to what rules were binding and what were not binding. The Conference found it impossible to arrive at an agreement on many of the most vital questions of maritime law. Under these circumstances the powers were not willing to have the proposed International Prize Court established without the previous codification of the body of law which was to govern its decisions.

In order to supply this need the London Naval Conference was convened in December, 1908, and issued a few months later the Declaration of London. The London Naval Conference was attended by representatives of the principal maritime powers including the United States, and the Declaration which it issued was avowedly a codification of the existing rules of international law. This was not true, however, of all the provisions of the Declaration. On several of the most vital questions of maritime law, such as blockade, the doctrine of continuous voyage, the destruction of neutral prizes, and the inclusion of food stuffs in the list of conditional contraband, the Declaration was a compromise and therefore unsatisfactory. It encountered from the start the most violent opposition in England. In Parliament the Naval Prize Bill, which was to give the Declaration effect, was discussed at considerable length. It passed the House of Commons by a small vote, but was defeated in the House of Lords. It was denounced by the press, and a petition to the king, drawn up by the Imperial Maritime League protesting against it, was signed by a long list of commercial associations, mayors, members of the House of Lords, general officers, and other public officials. One hundred and thirty-eight naval officers of flag rank addressed to the prime minister a public protest against the Declaration. In the debate in the House of Lords the main objections to the Declaration were (1) that it made food stuffs conditional contraband instead of placing them on the free list, (2) that the clause permitting the seizure of conditional contraband bound for a fortified place or "other place serving as a base for the armed forces of the enemy" would render all English ports liable to be treated as bases by an enemy, and (3) that it permitted the destruction of neutral prizes.

The refusal of England to ratify the Declaration of London sealed its fate. The United States Senate formally ratified it, but this ratification was, of course, conditional on the ratification of other powers. At the beginning of the Great War the United States made a formal proposal to the belligerent powers that they should agree to adopt the Declaration for the period of the war in order that there might be a definite body of law for all parties concerned. This proposal was accepted by Germany and Austria, but England, France, and Russia were not willing to accept the Declaration of London without modifications. The United States, therefore, promptly withdrew its proposal and stated that where its rights as a neutral were concerned it would expect the belligerent powers to observe the recognized rules of international law and existing treaties.

The Hague Conferences were concerned with questions of general international interest, and had no bearing upon the internal affairs of states. Such, however, was not the character of the conference which convened at Algeciras, Spain, in December, 1905, for the purpose of adjusting the very serious dispute that had arisen between France and Germany over the status of Morocco. France had been engaged for some years in the peaceful penetration of Morocco. By the terms of the Entente of 1904 England recognized Morocco as being within the French sphere of influence and France agreed to recognize England's position in Egypt. The German Kaiser had no idea of permitting any part of the world to be divided up without his consent. In March, 1905, while on a cruise in the Mediterranean, he disembarked at Tangier and paid a visit to the Sultan "in his character of independent sovereign." As the Russian armies had just suffered disastrous defeats at the hands of the Japanese, France could not count on aid from her ally and the Kaiser did not believe that the recently formed Entente was strong enough to enable her to count on English support. His object in landing at Tangier was, therefore, to check and humiliate France while she was isolated and to break up the Entente before it should develop into an alliance. Delcassé, the French foreign minister, wanted to stand firm, but Germany demanded his retirement and the prime minister accepted his resignation. In recognition of this triumph, the German chancellor Count von Bülow was given the title of Prince. Not satisfied with this achievement, the Kaiser demanded a general European conference on the Moroccan question, and, in order to avoid war, President Roosevelt persuaded France to submit the whole dispute to the powers interested. The Algeciras conference turned out to be a bitter disappointment to Germany. Not only did France receive the loyal support of England, but she was also backed by the United States and even by Italy—a warning to Germany that the Triple Alliance was in danger. As the conference was called nominally for the purpose of instituting certain administrative reforms in Morocco, President Roosevelt decided, in view of our rights under a commercial treaty of 1880, to take part in the proceedings. The American delegates were Henry White, at that time ambassador to Italy, and Samuel R. Gummeré, minister to Morocco. As the United States professed to have no political interests at stake, its delegates were instrumental in composing many of the difficulties that arose during the conference and their influence was exerted to preserve the European balance of power. The facts in regard to America's part in this conference were carefully concealed from the public. There was nothing in any published American document to indicate that the participation of our representatives was anything more than casual. André Tardieu, the well-known French publicist, who reported the conference and later published his impressions in book form, first indicated that President Roosevelt was a positive factor in the proceedings. But it was not until the publication of Bishop's "Theodore Roosevelt and His Time" that the full extent of Roosevelt's activities in this connection became known.

There can be no doubt that our participation in the Moroccan conference was the most radical departure ever made from our traditional policy of isolation. Roosevelt's influence was exerted for preserving the balance of power in Europe. As we look back upon the events of that year we feel, in view of what has since happened, that he was fully justified in the course he pursued. Had his motives for participating in the conference been known at the time, they would not have been upheld either by the Senate or by public opinion. There are many serious objections to secret diplomacy, but it cannot be entirely done away with even under a republican form of government until the people are educated to a fuller understanding of international politics. The German Kaiser was relentless in his attempt to score a diplomatic triumph while France was isolated. He was thwarted, however, by the moral support which England, Italy, and the United States gave to France.

During the proceedings of the conference the American delegates declared in open session that the United States had no political interest in Morocco and that they would sign the treaty only with the understanding that the United States would thereby assume no "obligation or responsibility for the enforcement thereof." This declaration did not satisfy the United States Senate, which no doubt suspected the part that was actually played by America in the conference. At any rate, when the treaty was finally ratified the Senate attached to its resolution of ratification the following declaration:

"Resolved further. That the Senate, as a part of this act of ratification, understands that the participation of the United States in the Algeciras conference and in the formation and adoption of the general act and protocol which resulted therefrom, was with the sole purpose of preserving and increasing its commerce in Morocco, the protection as to life, liberty, and property of its citizens residing or traveling therein, and of aiding by its friendly offices and efforts, in removing friction and controversy which seemed to menace the peace between powers signatory with the United States to the treaty of 1880, all of which are on terms of amity with this Government; and without purpose to depart from the traditional American foreign policy which forbids participation by the United States in the settlement of political questions which are entirely European in their scope."

The determination of the United States not to interfere in the internal politics of European States has not prevented occasional protests in the name of humanity against the harsh treatment accorded the Jews in certain European countries. On July 17, 1902, Secretary Hay protested in a note to the Rumanian government against a policy which was forcing thousands of Jews to emigrate from that country. The United States, he claimed, had more than a philanthropic interest in this matter, for the enforced emigration of the Jews from Rumania in a condition of utter destitution was "the mere transplantation of an artificially produced diseased growth to a new place"; and, as the United States was practically their only place of refuge, we had a clearly established right of remonstrance. In the case of Russia information has repeatedly been sought through diplomatic channels as to the extent of destitution among the Jewish population, and permission has been requested for the distribution of relief funds raised in the United

States. Such inquiries have been so framed as to amount to diplomatic protests. In his annual message of 1904 President Roosevelt went further and openly expressed the horror of the nation at the massacre of the Jews at Kishenef. These protests, however, were purely diplomatic in character. There was not the slightest hint at intervention. During the early stages of the Great War in Europe the Government of the United States endeavored to adhere strictly to its historic policy. The German invasion of Belgium with its attendant horrors made a deep impression upon the American people and aroused their fighting spirit even more perhaps than the German policy of submarine warfare, but it was on the latter issue, in which the interests and rights of the United States were directly involved, that we finally entered the war.

V

THE OPEN-DOOR POLICY

In the Orient American diplomacy has had a somewhat freer hand than in Europe. Commodore Perry's expedition to Japan in 1852-1854 was quite a radical departure from the general policy of attending strictly to our own business. It would hardly have been undertaken against a country lying within the European sphere of influence. There were, it is true, certain definite grievances to redress, but the main reason for the expedition was that Japan refused to recognize her obligations as a member of the family of nations and closed her ports to all intercourse with the outside world. American sailors who had been shipwrecked on the coast of Japan had failed to receive the treatment usually accorded by civilized nations. Finally the United States decided to send a naval force to Japan and to force that country to abandon her policy of exclusion and to open her ports to intercourse with other countries. Japan yielded only under the threat of superior force. The conduct of the expedition, as well as our subsequent diplomatic negotiations with Japan, was highly creditable to the United States, and the Japanese people later erected a monument to the memory of Perry on the spot where he first landed.

The acquisition of the Philippine Islands tended to bring us more fully into the current of world politics, but it did not necessarily disturb the balancing of European and American spheres as set up by President

Monroe. Various explanations have been given of President McKinley's decision to retain the Philippine group, but the whole truth has in all probability not yet been fully revealed. The partition of China through the establishment of European spheres of influence was well under way when the Philippine Islands came within our grasp. American commerce with China was at this time second to that of England alone, and the concessions which were being wrung from China by the European powers in such rapid succession presented a bad outlook for us. The United States could not follow the example of the powers of Europe, for the seizure of a sphere of influence in China would not have been supported by the Senate or upheld by public opinion. It is probable that President McKinley thought that the Philippine Islands would not only provide a market for American goods, which owing to the Dingley tariff were beginning to face retaliatory legislation abroad, but that they would provide a naval base which would be of great assistance in upholding our interests in China.

Talcott Williams made public some years later another explanation of President McKinley's decision which is interesting and appears to be well vouched for. He was informed by a member of McKinley's cabinet that while the President's mind was not yet made up on the question, a personal communication was received from Lord Salisbury who warned the President that Germany was preparing to take over the Philippine Islands in case the United States should withdraw; that such a step would probably precipitate a world war and that in the interests of peace and harmony it would be best for the United States to retain the entire group.

The famous open-door policy was outlined by Secretary Hay in notes dated September 6, 1899, addressed to Great Britain, Germany, and Russia. Each of these powers was requested to give assurance and to make a declaration to the following effect: (1) that it would not interfere with any treaty port or vested interests in its so-called sphere of influence; (2) that it would permit the Chinese tariff to continue in force in such sphere and to be collected by Chinese officials; (3) that it would not discriminate against other foreigners in the matter of port dues or railroad rates. Similar notes were later addressed to France, Italy, and Japan. England alone expressed her willingness to sign such a declaration. The other powers, while professing thorough accord with the principles set forth by Mr. Hay, avoided committing themselves to a formal declaration and no such declaration was ever made. Mr. Hay made a skillful move, however, to clinch matters by informing each of the powers to whom the note had been addressed that in view of the favorable replies from the other powers, its acceptance of the proposals of the United States was considered "as final and definitive."

Americans generally are under the impression that John Hay originated the open-door policy and that it was successfully upheld by the United States. Neither of these impressions is correct. A few months before John Hay formulated his famous note Lord Charles Beresford came through America on his return from China and addressed the leading chambers of commerce from San Francisco to New York, telling Americans what was actually taking place in China and urging this country to unite with England and Japan in an effort to maintain the open door. Like the Monroe Doctrine, the open-door policy was thus Anglo-American in origin. There is little doubt that England and Japan were willing to form an alliance with the United States for the purpose of maintaining the open door in China, but our traditional policy of isolation prevented our committing ourselves to the employment of force. President McKinley, following the example of President Monroe, preferred announcing our policy independently and requesting the other powers to consent to it. Had John Hay been able to carry out the plan which he favored of an alliance with England and Japan, the mere announcement of the fact would have been sufficient to check the aggressions of the powers in China. Instead of such an alliance, however, we let it be known that while we favored the open door we would not fight for it under any conditions.

The utter worthlessness of the replies that were made in response to Hay's note of September 6, 1899, became fully apparent in the discussions that soon arose as to the status of consuls in the various spheres of influence. Japan claimed that sovereignty did not pass with a lease and that even if China should surrender jurisdiction over her own people, the lessee governments could not acquire jurisdiction over foreigners in leased territory. This position was undoubtedly correct if the territorial integrity of China was really to be preserved, but after negotiations with Russia and the other powers concerned Mr. Hay wrote to Minister Conger on February 3, 1900, that "The United States consuls in districts adjacent to the foreign leased territories are to be instructed that they have no authority to exercise extra-territorial consular jurisdiction or to perform ordinary non-judicial consular acts within the leased territory under their present Chinese exequaturs." Application was then made to the European powers for the admission of American consuls in the leased territories for the performance of the ordinary consular functions, but in no case were they to exercise extra-territorial jurisdiction within a leased territory.

The exploitation of China which continued at a rapid rate naturally aroused an intense anti-foreign sentiment and led to the Boxer uprising. Events moved with startling rapidity and United States troops took a prominent part with those of England, France, Russia, and Japan in the march to Peking for the relief of the legations. In a note to the powers July 3, 1900, Secretary Hay, in defining the attitude of the United States on the Chinese question, said: "The policy of the government of the United States is to seek a solution which may bring about permanent safety and peace to China, preserve Chinese territorial and administrative entity, protect all rights guaranteed to friendly powers by treaty and international law, and safeguard for the world the principle of equal and impartial trade with all parts of the Chinese empire." Mr. Hay's notes were skillfully worded and had some influence in helping to formulate public opinion on the Chinese question both in this country and abroad, but we know now from his private letters which have recently been made public that he realized only too fully the utter futility of his efforts to stay the course of events. During the exciting days of June, 1900, when the foreign legations at Peking were in a state of siege, Mr. Hay wrote to John W. Foster as follows:

"What can be done in the present diseased state of the public mind? There is such a mad-dog hatred of England prevalent among newspapers and politicians that anything we should now do in China to take care of our imperiled interests would be set down to 'subservience to Great Britain'.... Every Senator I see says, 'For God's sake, don't let it appear we have any understanding with England.' How can I make bricks without straw? That we should be compelled to refuse the assistance of the greatest power in the world, in carrying out our own policy, because all Irishmen are Democrats and some Germans are fools—is enough to drive a man mad. Yet we shall do what we can."

A little later (September 20, 1900) in confidential letters to Henry Adams, he exclaimed:

"About China, it is the devil's own mess. We cannot possibly publish all the facts without breaking off relations with several Powers. We shall have to do the best we can, and take the consequences, which will be pretty serious, I do not doubt. 'Give and take'—the axiom of diplomacy to the rest of the world—is positively forbidden to us, by both the Senate and public opinion. We must take what we can and give nothing—which greatly narrows our possibilities.

"I take it, you agree with us that we are to limit as far as possible our military operations in China, to withdraw our troops at the earliest day consistent with our obligations, and in the final adjustment to do everything we can for the integrity and reform of China, and to hold on like grim death to the Open Door. . . ."

Again, November 21, 1900:

"What a business this has been in China! So far we have got on by being honest and naïf. . . . At least we are spared the infamy of an alliance with Germany. I would rather, I think, be the dupe of China, than the chum of the Kaiser. Have you noticed how the world will take anything nowadays from a German? Bülow said yesterday in substance—'We have demanded of China everything we can think of. If we think of anything else we will demand that, and be d—d to you'—and not a man in the world kicks."

During the long negotiations that followed the occupation of Peking by the powers, the United States threw the weight of its influence on the side of moderation, urging the powers not to impose too many burdens on China and declaring that the only hope for the future lay in a strong, independent, responsible Chinese government. Contrary to the terms of the final protocol, however, Russia retained in Manchuria the troops concentrated there during the Boxer movement with a view to exacting further concessions from China. The open-door policy was again ignored. The seriousness of the situation led England and Japan to sign a defensive agreement January 30, 1902, recognizing England's interest in China and Japan's interest in Korea, and providing that if either party should be attacked in defense of its interest, the other party would remain neutral, unless a third power joined in, in which event the second party would come to the assistance of the first. A formal protest made by the United States, February 1, against some of the demands Russia was making on China led

Russia to conclude that the American government had an understanding with England and Japan, but Mr. Hay gave the assurance that he had known nothing about the Anglo-Japanese agreement until it was made public. He succeeded in securing from Russia, however, a definite promise to evacuate Manchuria, but as the time for the withdrawal of her troops drew near, Russia again imposed new conditions on China, and deliberately misrepresented to the United States the character of the new proposals.

After the suppression of the Boxer uprising, China had agreed to extend the scope of her commercial treaties with the powers. When the negotiation of a new treaty with the United States was begun, our representative demanded that at least two new ports in Manchuria be opened to foreign trade and residence. The Chinese commissioners declined to discuss the subject on the alleged ground that they had no instructions to do so. It was evident that there was secret opposition somewhere, and after considerable difficulty Mr. Hay finally secured evidence that it came from Russia. When confronted with the evidence the Russian Government finally admitted the facts. We were told that we could not be admitted to one of the ports that we had designated because it was situated within the Russian railway zone, and therefore not under the complete jurisdiction of China, but that another port would be substituted for it. Secretary Hay and President Roosevelt were helpless. They accepted what they could get and kept quiet. "The administrative entity" of China was again utterly ignored. The difficulty was that we did not have a strong enough navy in the Pacific to fight Russia alone, and President Roosevelt and Secretary Hay realized that neither the Senate nor public opinion would consent to an alliance with England and Japan. Had these three powers made a joint declaration in support of the open-door policy, the exploitation of China would have ceased, there would have been no Russo-Japanese war, and the course of world history during the period that has since intervened might have been very different.

When we backed down and abandoned Manchuria to Russian exploitation Japan stepped into the breach. After long negotiations the Japanese Government finally delivered an ultimatum to Russia which resulted in the rupture of diplomatic relations and war. After a series of notable victories on land and sea Japan was fast approaching the end of her resources, and it is now an open secret that the Emperor wrote a personal letter to President Roosevelt requesting him to intervene diplomatically and pave the way for peace. The President was quick to act on the suggestion and the commissioners of Russia and Japan met at Portsmouth, New Hampshire. Here President Roosevelt's intervention should have ceased. The terms of the Treaty of Portsmouth were a bitter disappointment to the Japanese people and the Japanese commissioners undertook to shift the burden from their shoulders by stating that President Roosevelt had urged them to surrender their claim to the Island of Saghalien and to give up all idea of an indemnity. Japanese military triumph had again, as at the close of the Chino-Japanese War, been followed by diplomatic defeat, and for this defeat Japanese public opinion held President Roosevelt responsible. From the days of Commodore Perry and Townsend Harris to the Treaty of Portsmouth, relations between the United States and Japan had been almost ideal. Since the negotiations at Portsmouth there has been a considerable amount of bad feeling, and at times diplomatic relations have been subjected to a severe strain.

Having fought a costly war in order to check the Russian advance in Manchuria, the Japanese naturally felt that they had a paramount interest in China. They consequently sharply resented the attempts which the United States subsequently made, particularly Secretary Knox's proposal for the neutralization of the railways of Manchuria, to formulate policies for China. They took the position that we had had our day and that we must henceforth remain hands off so far as China was concerned. This attitude of mind was not unnatural and during the World War the United States, in order to bind the Japanese government more closely to the Allied Cause, agreed to recognize, in the Lansing-Ishii agreement, the "special interests" of Japan in China.

VI

ANGLO-AMERICAN RELATIONS

A few years ago George L. Beer, one of our leading students of British colonial policy, said "It is easily conceivable, and not at all improbable, that the political evolution of the next centuries may take such a course that the American Revolution will lose the great significance that is now attached to it, and will appear merely as the temporary separation of two kindred peoples whose inherent similarity was obscured by superficial differences resulting from dissimilar economic and social conditions." This statement does not appear as extravagant to-day as it did ten years ago. As early as 1894, Captain Mahan, the great authority on naval history, published an essay entitled "Possibilities of an Anglo-American Reunion," in which he pointed out that these two countries were the only great powers which were by geographical position exempt from the burden of large armies and dependent upon the sea for intercourse with the other great nations.

In a volume dealing with questions of American foreign policy, published in 1907, the present writer concluded the last paragraph with this statement: "By no means the least significant of recent changes is the development of cordial relations with England; and it seems now that the course of world politics is destined to lead to the further reknitting together of the two great branches of the Anglo-Saxon race in bonds of peace and international sympathy, in a union not cemented by any formal alliance, but based on community of interests and of aims, a union that will constitute the highest guarantee of the political stability and moral progress of the world."

The United States has very naturally had closer contact with England than with any other European power. This has been due to the fact that England was the mother country, that after independence was established a large part of our trade continued to be with the British Isles, that our northern boundary touches British territory for nearly four thousand miles, and that the British navy and mercantile marine have dominated the Atlantic Ocean which has been our chief highway of intercourse with other nations. Having had more points of contact we have had more disputes with England than with any other nation. Some writers have half jocularly attributed this latter fact to our common language. The Englishman reads our books, papers, and magazines, and knows what we think of him, while we read what he writes about us, and in neither case is the resulting impression flattering to the national pride.

Any one who takes the trouble to read what was written in England about America and the Americans between 1820 and 1850 will wonder how war was avoided. A large number of English travellers came to the United States during this period and published books about us when they got home. The books were bad enough in themselves, but the great English periodicals, the *Edinburgh Review, Blackwood's,* the *British Review,* and the *Quarterly,* quoted at length the most objectionable passages from these writers and made malicious attacks on Americans and American institutions. American men were described as "turbulent citizens, abandoned Christians, inconstant husbands, unnatural fathers, and treacherous friends." Our soldiers and sailors were charged with cowardice in the War of 1812. It was stated that "in the southern parts of the Union the rites of our holy faith are almost never practised. . . . Three and a half millions enjoy no means of religious instruction. The religious principle is gaining ground in the northern parts of the Union; it is becoming fashionable among the better orders of society to go to church . . . The greater number of states declare it to be unconstitutional to refer to the providence of God in any of their public acts." The *Quarterly Review* informed its readers that "the supreme felicity of a true-born American is inaction of body and inanity of mind." Dickens's *American Notes* was an ungrateful return for the kindness and enthusiasm with which he had been received in this country. De Tocqueville's *Democracy in America* was widely read in England and doubtless had its influence in revising opinion concerning America. Richard Cobden was, however, the first Englishman to interpret correctly the significance of America as an economic force. His essay on America, published in 1835, pointed out that British policy should be more concerned with economic relations with America than with European politics. As Professor Dunning says, "Cobden made the United States the text of his earliest sermon against militarism and protectionism."

Notwithstanding innumerable disputes over boundaries, fisheries, and fur seals, trade with the British West Indies and Canada, and questions of neutral rights and obligations, we have had unbroken peace for more than a hundred years. Upon several occasions, notably during the Canadian insurrection of 1837 and during our own Civil War, disturbances along the Canadian border created strained relations, but absence of frontier guards and forts has prevented hasty action on the part of either government. The agreement of 1817, effecting disarmament on the Great Lakes, has not only saved both countries the enormous cost of maintaining navies on these inland waters, but it has prevented hostile demonstrations in times of crisis.

During the Canadian rebellion of 1837 Americans along the border expressed openly their sympathy for the insurgents who secured arms and munitions from the American side. In December a British force crossed the Niagara River, boarded and took possession of the *Caroline*, a vessel which had been hired by the insurgents to convey their cannon and other supplies. The ship was fired and sent over the Falls. When the *Caroline* was boarded one American, Amos Durfee, was killed and several others wounded. The United States at once demanded redress, but the British Government took the position that the seizure of the *Caroline* was a justifiable act of self-defense against people whom their own government either could not or would not control.

The demands of the United States were still unredressed when in 1840 a Canadian named Alexander McLeod made the boast in a tavern on the American side that he had slain Durfee. He was taken at his word, examined before a magistrate, and committed to jail in Lockport. McLeod's arrest created great excitement on both sides of the border. The British minister at Washington called upon the Government of the United States "to take prompt and effectual steps for the liberation of Mr. McLeod." Secretary of State Forsyth replied that the offense with which McLeod was charged had been committed within the State of New York; that the jurisdiction of each State of the United States was, within its proper sphere, perfectly independent of the Federal Government; that the latter could not interfere. The date set for the trial of McLeod was the fourth Monday in March, 1841. Van Buren's term ended and Harrison's began on the 4th of March, and Webster became Secretary of State. The British minister was given instructions by his government to demand the immediate release of McLeod. This demand was made, he said, because the attack on the *Caroline* was an act of a public character; because it was a justifiable use of force for the defense of British territory against unprovoked attack by "British rebels and American pirates"; because it was contrary to the principles of civilized nations to hold individuals responsible for acts done by order of the constituted authorities of the State; and because Her Majesty's government could not admit the doctrine that the Federal Government had no power to interfere and that the decision must rest with the State of New York. The relations of foreign powers were with the Federal Government. To admit that the Federal Government had no control over a State would lead to the dissolution of the Union so far as foreign powers were concerned, and to the accrediting of foreign diplomatic agents, not to the Federal Government, but to each separate State. Webster received the note quietly and sent the attorney-general to Lockport to see that McLeod had competent counsel. After considerable delay, during which Webster replied to the main arguments of the British note, McLeod was acquitted and released.

In the midst of the dispute over the case of the *Caroline* serious trouble arose between the authorities of Maine and New Brunswick over the undetermined boundary between the St. Croix River and the Highlands, and there ensued the so-called "Aroostook War." During the summer of 1838 British and American lumbermen began operating along the Aroostook River in large numbers. The governor of Maine sent a body of militia to enforce the authority of that State, and the New Brunswick authorities procured a detachment of British regulars to back up their position. Bloodshed was averted by the arrival of General Winfield Scott, who managed to restrain the Maine authorities. The administration found it necessary to take up seriously the settlement of the boundary question, and for the next three years the matter was under consideration, while each side had surveyors employed in a vain attempt to locate a line which would correspond to the line of the treaty. As soon as the McLeod affair was settled, Webster devoted himself earnestly to the boundary question. He decided to drop the mass of data accumulated by the surveyors and historians, and to reach an agreement by direct negotiation.

In April, 1842, Alexander Baring, Lord Ashburton, arrived in Washington and the following August the Webster-Ashburton treaty was signed. The boundary fixed by the treaty gave Maine a little more than half the area which she claimed and the United States appropriated $150,000 to compensate Maine for the territory which she had lost.

The settlement of these matters did not, however, insure peace with England. Settlers were crowding into Oregon and it was evident that the joint occupation, established by the convention of 1818, would soon have to be terminated and a divisional line agreed upon. Great Britain insisted that her southern boundary should extend at least as far as the Columbia River, while Americans finally claimed the whole of the disputed area, and one of the slogans of the presidential campaign of 1844 was "Fifty-Four-Forty or Fight." At the same time Great Britain actively opposed the annexation of Texas by the United States. Her main reason for this course was that she wished to encourage the development of Texas as a cotton-growing country from which she could draw a large enough supply to make her independent of the United States. If Texas should thus devote herself to the production of cotton as her chief export crop, she would, of course, adopt a free-trade policy and thus create a considerable market for British goods.

As soon as it became evident that Tyler contemplated taking definite steps toward annexation, Lord Aberdeen secured the coöperation of the government of Louis Philippe in opposing the absorption of Texas by the American republic. While the treaty for the annexation of Texas was before the Senate, Lord Aberdeen came forward with a proposition that England and France should unite with Texas and Mexico in a diplomatic act or perpetual treaty, securing to Texas recognition as an independent republic, but preventing her from ever acquiring territory beyond the Rio Grande or joining the American union. While the United States would be invited to join in this act, it was not expected that the government of that country would agree to it. Mexico obstinately refused to recognize the independence of Texas. Lord Aberdeen was so anxious to prevent the annexation of Texas that he was ready, if supported by France, to coerce Mexico and fight the

United States, but the French Government was not willing to go this far, so the scheme was abandoned.

The two foremost issues in the campaign of 1844 were the annexation of Texas and the occupation of Oregon. Texas was annexed by joint resolution a few days before the inauguration of Polk. This act, it was foreseen, would probably provoke a war with Mexico, so Polk's first task was to adjust the Oregon dispute in order to avoid complications with England. The fate of California was also involved. That province was not likely to remain long in the hands of a weak power like Mexico. In fact, British consular agents and naval officers had for several years been urging upon their government the great value of Upper California. Aberdeen refused to countenance any insurrectionary movement in California, but he directed his agents to keep vigilant watch on the proceedings of citizens of the United States in that province. Had England and Mexico arrived at an understanding and joined in a war against the United States, the probabilities are that England would have acquired not only the whole of Oregon, but California besides. In fact, in May, 1846, just as we were on the point of going to war with Mexico, the president of Mexico officially proposed to transfer California to England as security for a loan. Fortunately, the Oregon question had been adjusted and England had no reason for wishing to go to war with the United States. Mexico's offer was therefore rejected. Polk managed the diplomatic situation with admirable promptness and firmness. Notwithstanding the fact that the democratic platform had demanded "Fifty-Four-Forty or Fight," as soon as Polk became President he offered to compromise with England on the 49th parallel. When this offer was declined he asked permission of Congress to give England the necessary notice for the termination of the joint occupation agreement, to provide for the military defense of the territory in dispute, and to extend over it the laws of the United States. A few months later notice was given to England, but at the same time the hope was expressed that the matter might be adjusted diplomatically. As soon as it was evident that the United States was in earnest, England gracefully yielded and accepted the terms which had been first proposed.

As war with Mexico was imminent the public generally approved of the Oregon compromise, though the criticism was made by some in the North that the South, having secured in Texas a large addition to slave territory, was indifferent about the expansion of free territory. In fact, Henry Cabot Lodge, in his recent little book, "One Hundred Years of Peace," says: "The loss of the region between the forty-ninth parallel and the line of 54-40 was one of the most severe which ever befell the United States. Whether it could have been obtained without a war is probably doubtful, but it never ought to have been said, officially or otherwise, that we would fight for 54-40 unless we were fully prepared to do so. If we had stood firm for the line of 54-40 without threats, it is quite possible that we might have succeeded in the end; but the hypotheses of history are of little practical value, and the fact remains that by the treaty of 1846 we lost a complete control of the Pacific coast."

That the United States lived through what Professor Dunning calls "the roaring forties" without a war with England seems now little less than a miracle. During the next fifteen years relations were much more amicable, though by no means free from disputes. The most important diplomatic act was the signature in 1850 of the Clayton-Bulwer treaty which conceded to England a joint interest in any canal that might be built through the isthmus connecting North and South America. One of the interesting episodes of this period was the dismissal of Crampton, the British minister, who insisted on enlisting men in the United States for service in the Crimean War, an act which pales into insignificance in comparison with some of the things which Bernstorff did during the early stages of the Great War.

Relations between the United States and England during the American Civil War involved so many highly technical questions that it is impossible to do more than touch upon them in the present connection. Diplomatic discussions centred about such questions as the validity of the blockade established by President Lincoln, the recognition by England of Confederate belligerency, the *Trent* affair, and the responsibility of England for the depredations committed by the *Alabama* and other Confederate cruisers. When the United States first demanded reparation for the damage inflicted on American commerce by the Confederate cruisers, the British Government disclaimed all liability on the ground that the fitting out of the cruisers had not been completed within British jurisdiction. Even after the close of the war the British Government continued to reject all proposals for a settlement. The American nation, flushed with victory, was bent on redress, and so deep-seated was the resentment against England, that the Fenian movement, which had for its object the establishment of an independent republic in Ireland, met with open encouragement in this country. The House of Representatives went so far as to repeal the law forbidding Americans to fit out ships for belligerents, but the Senate failed to concur. The successful war waged by Prussia against Austria in 1866 disturbed the European balance, and rumblings of the approaching Franco-Prussian war caused uneasiness in British cabinet circles. Fearing that if Great Britain were drawn into the conflict the American people might take a sweet revenge by fitting out "Alabamas" for her enemies, the British Government assumed a more conciliatory attitude, and in January, 1869, Lord Clarendon signed with Reverdy Johnson a convention providing for the submission to a mixed commission of all claims which had arisen since 1853. Though the convention included, it did not specifically mention, the *Alabama* Claims, and it failed to contain any expression of regret for the course pursued by the British Government during the war. The Senate, therefore, refused by an almost unanimous vote to ratify the arrangement.

When Grant became President, Hamilton Fish renewed the negotiations through Motley, the American minister at London, but the latter was unduly influenced by the extreme views of Sumner, chairman of the Senate committee on foreign relations, to whose influence he owed his appointment, and got things in a bad tangle. Fish then transferred the negotiations to Washington, where a joint high commission, appointed to settle the various disputes with Canada, convened in 1871. A few months later the treaty of Washington was signed. Among other things it provided for submitting the *Alabama* Claims to an arbitration tribunal composed of five members, one appointed by England, one by the United States, and the other three by the rulers of Italy, Switzerland, and Brazil. When this tribunal met at Geneva, the following year, the United States, greatly to the surprise of everybody, presented not only the direct claims for the damage inflicted by the Confederate cruisers, but also indirect claims for the loss sustained through the transfer of American shipping to foreign flags, for the prolongation of the war, and for increased rates of insurance. Great Britain threatened to withdraw from the arbitration, but Charles Francis Adams, the American member of the tribunal, rose nobly to the occasion and decided against the contention of his own government. The indirect claims were rejected by a unanimous vote and on the direct claims the United States was awarded the sum of $15,500,000. Although the British member of the tribunal dissented from the decision his government promptly paid the award. This was the most important case that had ever been submitted to arbitration and its successful adjustment encouraged the hope that the two great branches of the English-speaking peoples would never again have to resort to war.

Between the settlement of the *Alabama* Claims and the controversy over the Venezuelan boundary, diplomatic intercourse between the two countries was enlivened by the efforts of Blaine and Frelinghuysen to convince the British Government that the Clayton-Bulwer treaty was out of date and therefore no longer binding, by the assertion of American ownership in the seal herds of Bering Sea and the attempt to prevent Canadians from taking these animals in the open sea, and by the summary dismissal of Lord Sackville-West, the third British minister to receive his passports from the United States without request.

President Cleveland's bold assertion of the Monroe Doctrine in the Venezuelan boundary dispute, while the subject of much criticism at the time both at home and abroad, turned out to be a most opportune assertion of the intention of the United States to protect the American continents from the sort of exploitation to which Africa and Asia have fallen a prey, and, strange to say, it had a clarifying effect on our relations with England, whose attitude has since been uniformly friendly.

The Venezuelan affair was followed by the proposal of Lord Salisbury to renew the negotiations for a permanent treaty of arbitration which had been first entered into by Secretary Gresham and Sir Julian Pauncefote. In the spring of 1890 the Congress of the United States had adopted a resolution in favor of the negotiation of arbitration treaties with friendly nations, and the British House of Commons had in July, 1893, expressed its hearty approval of a general arbitration treaty between the United States and England. The matter was then taken up diplomatically, as stated above, but was dropped when the Venezuelan boundary dispute became acute. Lord Salisbury's proposal was favorably received by President Cleveland, and after mature deliberation the draft of a treaty was finally drawn up and signed by Secretary Olney and Sir Julian Pauncefote. This treaty provided for the submission of pecuniary claims to the familiar mixed commission with an umpire or referee to decide disputed points. Controversies involving the determination of territorial claims were to be submitted to a tribunal composed of six members, three justices of the Supreme Court of the United States or judges of the Circuit Court to be nominated by the president of the United States, and three judges of the British Supreme Court of Judicature or members of the Judicial Committee of the Privy Council to be nominated by the British sovereign, and an award made by a majority of not less than five to one was to be final. In case of an award made by less than the prescribed majority, the award was also to be final unless either power should within three months protest against it, in which case the award was to be of no validity. This treaty was concluded in January, 1897, and promptly submitted to the Senate. When President Cleveland's term expired in March no action had been taken. President McKinley endorsed the treaty in his inaugural address and urged the Senate to take prompt action, but when the vote was taken, May 5th, it stood forty-three for, and twenty-six against, the treaty. It thus lacked three votes of the two thirds required for ratification. The failure of this treaty was a great disappointment to the friends of international arbitration. The opposition within his own party to President Cleveland, under whose direction the treaty had been negotiated, and the change of administration, probably had a good deal to do with its defeat. Public opinion, especially in the Northern States of the Union, was still hostile to England. Irish agitators could always get a sympathetic hearing in America, and politicians could not resist the temptation to play on anti-British prejudices in order to bring out the Irish vote.

The Spanish War was the turning point in our relations with England as in many other things. The question as to who were our friends in 1898 was much discussed at the time, and when revived by the press upon the occasion of the visit of Prince Henry of Prussia to the United States in February, 1902, even the cabinets of Europe could not refrain from taking part in the controversy. In order to diminish the enthusiasm over the Prince's visit the British press circulated the story that Lord Pauncefote had checked a movement of the European powers to prevent any intervention of the United States in Cuba; while the German papers asserted that Lord

Pauncefote had taken the initiative in opposing American intervention. It is certain that the attitude of the British Government, as well as of the British people, from the outbreak of hostilities to the close of the war, was friendly. As for Germany, while the conduct of the government was officially correct, public sentiment expressed itself with great violence against the United States. The conduct of the German admiral, Diederichs, in Manila Bay has never been satisfactorily explained. Shortly after Dewey's victory a German squadron, superior to the American in strength, steamed into the Bay and displayed, according to Dewey, an "extraordinary disregard of the usual courtesies of naval intercourse." Dewey finally sent his flag-lieutenant, Brumby, to inform the German admiral that "if he wants a fight he can have it right now." The German admiral at once apologized. It is well known now that the commander of the British squadron, which was in a position to bring its guns to bear on the Germans, gave Dewey to understand that he could rely on more than moral support from him in case of trouble. In fact, John Hay wrote from London at the beginning of the war that the British navy was at our disposal for the asking.

Great Britain's change of attitude toward the United States was so marked that some writers have naïvely concluded that a secret treaty of alliance between the two countries was made in 1897. The absurdity of such a statement was pointed out by Senator Lodge several years ago. England's change of attitude is not difficult to understand. For a hundred years after the battle of Trafalgar, England had pursued the policy of maintaining a navy large enough to meet all comers. With the rapid growth of other navies during the closing years of the nineteenth century, England realized that she could no longer pursue this policy. Russia, Japan, and Germany had all adopted extensive naval programs when we went to war with Spain. Our acquisition of the Philippines and Porto Rico and our determination to build an isthmian canal made a large American navy inevitable. Great Britain realized, therefore, that she would have to cast about for future allies. She therefore signed the Hay-Pauncefote Treaty with us in 1901, and a defensive alliance with Japan in 1902.

In view of the fact that the United States was bent on carrying out the long-deferred canal scheme, Great Britain realized that a further insistence on her rights under the Clayton-Bulwer Treaty would lead to friction and possible conflict. She wisely decided, therefore, to recede from the position which she had held for half a century and to give us a free hand in the construction and control of the canal at whatever point we might choose to build it. While the Hay-Pauncefote treaty was limited in terms to the canal question, it was in reality of much wider significance. It amounted, in fact, to the recognition of American naval supremacy in the West Indies, and since its signature Great Britain has withdrawn her squadron from this important strategic area. The supremacy of the United States in the Caribbean is now firmly established and in fact unquestioned. The American public did not appreciate at the time the true significance of the Hay-Pauncefote Treaty, and a few years later Congress inserted in the Panama Tolls Act a clause exempting American ships engaged in the coastwise trade from the payment of tolls. Great Britain at once protested against the exemption clause as a violation of the Hay-Pauncefote Treaty and anti-British sentiment at once flared up in all parts of the United States. Most American authorities on international law and diplomacy believed that Great Britain's interpretation of the treaty was correct. Fortunately President Wilson took the same view, and in spite of strong opposition he persuaded Congress to repeal the exemption clause. This was an act of simple justice and it removed the only outstanding subject of dispute between the two countries.

The Hay-Pauncefote Treaty was by no means the only evidence of a change of attitude on the part of Great Britain. As we have already seen, Great Britain and the United States were in close accord during the Boxer uprising in China and the subsequent negotiations. During the Russo-Japanese war public sentiment in both England and the United States was strongly in favor of Japan. At the Algeciras conference on Moroccan affairs in 1905 the United States, in its effort to preserve the European balance of power, threw the weight of its influence on the side of England and France.

The submission of the Alaskan boundary dispute to a form of arbitration in which Canada could not win and we could not lose was another evidence of the friendly attitude of Great Britain. The boundary between the southern strip of Alaska and British Columbia had never been marked or even accurately surveyed when gold was discovered in the Klondike. The shortest and quickest route to the gold-bearing region was by the trails leading up from Dyea and Skagway on the headwaters of Lynn Canal. The Canadian officials at once advanced claims to jurisdiction over these village ports. The question turned on the treaty made in 1825 between Great Britain and Russia. Whatever rights Russia had under that treaty we acquired by the purchase of Alaska in 1867. Not only did a long series of maps issued by the Canadian government in years past confirm the American claim to the region in dispute, but the correspondence of the British negotiator of the treaty of 1825 shows that he made every effort to secure for England an outlet to deep water through this strip of territory and failed. Under the circumstances President Roosevelt was not willing to submit the case to the arbitration of third parties. He agreed, however, to submit it to a mixed commission composed of three Americans, two Canadians, and Lord Alverstone, chief justice of England. As there was little doubt as to the views that would be taken by the three Americans and the two Canadians it was evident from the first that the trial was really before Lord Alverstone. In case he sustained the American contention there would be an end of the controversy; in case he sustained the Canadian view, there would be an even division, and matters would stand where they stood when the trial began except that a great deal more feeling would have been engendered and the United States might have had to make good its claims by force. Fortunately Lord Alverstone agreed with the three Americans on the main points involved in the controversy. The decision was, of course, a disappointment to the Canadians and it was charged that Lord Alverstone had sacrificed their interest in order to further the British policy of friendly relations with the United States.

At the beginning of the Great War the interference of the British navy with cargoes consigned to Germany at once aroused the latent anti-British feeling in this country. Owing to the fact that cotton exports were so largely involved the feeling against Great Britain was even stronger in the Southern States than in the Northern. The State Department promptly protested against the naval policy adopted by Great Britain, and the dispute might have assumed very serious proportions had not Germany inaugurated her submarine campaign. The dispute with England involved merely property rights, while that with Germany involved the safety and lives of American citizens. The main feature of British policy, that is, her application of the doctrine of continuous voyage, was so thoroughly in line with the policy adopted by the United States during the Civil War that the protests of our State Department were of little avail. In fact Great Britain merely carried the American doctrine to its logical conclusions.

We have undertaken in this brief review of Anglo-American relations to outline the more important controversies that have arisen between the two countries. They have been sufficiently numerous and irritating to jeopardize seriously the peace which has so happily subsisted for one hundred years between the two great members of the English-speaking family. After all, they have not been based on any fundamental conflict of policy, but have been for the most part superficial and in many cases the result of bad manners. In this connection Lord Bryce makes the following interesting observations:

"There were moments when the stiff and frigid attitude of the British foreign secretary exasperated the American negotiators, or when a demagogic Secretary of State at Washington tried by a bullying tone to win credit as the patriotic champion of national claims. But whenever there were bad manners in London there was good temper at Washington, and when there was a storm on the Potomac there was calm on the Thames. It was the good fortune of the two countries that if at any moment rashness or vehemence was found on one side, it never happened to be met by the like quality on the other."

"The moral of the story of Anglo-American relations," Lord Bryce says, "is that peace can always be kept, whatever be the grounds of controversy, between peoples that wish to keep it." He adds that Great Britain and the United States "have given the finest example ever seen in history of an undefended frontier, along which each people has trusted to the good faith of the other that it would create no naval armaments; and this very absence of armaments has itself helped to prevent hostile demonstrations. Neither of them has ever questioned the sanctity of treaties, or denied that states are bound by the moral law."

It is not strange that so many controversies about more or less trivial matters should have obscured in the minds of both Englishmen and Americans the fundamental identity of aim and purpose in the larger things of life. For notwithstanding the German influence in America which has had an undue part in shaping our educational methods, our civilization is still English. Bismarck realized this when he said that one of the most significant facts in modern history was that all North America was English-speaking. Our fundamental ideals are the same. We have a passion for liberty; we uphold the rights of the individual as against the extreme claims of the state; we believe in government through public opinion; we believe in the rule of law; we believe in government limited by fundamental principles and constitutional restraints as against the exercise of arbitrary power; we have never been subjected to militarism or to the dominance of a military caste; we are both so situated geographically as to be dependent on sea power rather than on large armies, and not only do navies not endanger the liberty of peoples but they are negligible quantities politically. Great Britain had in 1914 only 137,500 officers and men in her navy and 26,200 reserves, a wholly insignificant number compared to the millions that formed the army of Germany and gave a military color to the whole life and thought of the nation.

Not only are our political ideals the same, but in general our attitude toward world politics is the same, and most people are surprised when they are told that our fundamental foreign policies are identical. The two most characteristic American foreign policies, the Monroe Doctrine and the Open Door, were both, as we have seen, Anglo-American in origin.

VII

IMPERIALISTIC TENDENCIES OF THE MONROE DOCTRINE

In its original form the Monroe Doctrine was a direct defiance of Europe, and it has never been favorably regarded by the nations of the old world. Latterly, however, it has encountered adverse criticism in some of the Latin-American states whose independence it helped to secure and whose freedom from European control it has been instrumental in maintaining. The Latin-American attacks on the Doctrine during the last few years have been reflected to a greater or less extent by writers in this country, particularly in academic circles. The American writer who has become most conspicuous in this connection is Professor Bingham of Yale, who has travelled extensively in South America and who published in 1913 a little volume entitled "The Monroe Doctrine, an Obsolete Shibboleth." The reasons why the Monroe Doctrine has called forth so much criticism during the last few years are not far to seek. The rapid advance of the United States in the Caribbean Sea since 1898 has naturally aroused the apprehensions of the feebler Latin-American states in that region, while the building of the Panama Canal has rendered inevitable the adoption of a policy of naval supremacy in the Caribbean and has led to the formulation of new political policies in the zone of the Caribbean—what Admiral Chester calls the larger Panama Canal Zone—that is, the West Indies, Mexico and Central America, Colombia and Venezuela. Some of these policies, which have already been formulated to a far greater extent than is generally realized, are the establishment of protectorates, the supervision of finances, the control of all available canal routes, the acquisition of coaling stations, and the policing of disorderly countries.

The long-delayed advance of the United States in the Caribbean Sea actually began with the Spanish War. Since then we have made rapid strides. Porto Rico was annexed at the close of the war, and Cuba became a protectorate; the Canal Zone was a little later leased on terms that amounted to practical annexation, and the Dominican Republic came under the financial supervision of the United States; President Wilson went further and assumed the administration of Haitian affairs, leased from Nicaragua for a term of ninety-nine years a naval base on Fonseca Bay, and purchased the Danish West Indies. As a result of this rapid extension of American influence the political relations of the countries bordering on the Caribbean will of necessity be profoundly affected. Our Latin-American policy has been enlarged in meaning and limited in territorial application so far as its newer phases are concerned.

In 1904 President Roosevelt made a radical departure from our traditional policy in proposing that we should assume financial supervision over the Dominican Republic in order to prevent certain European powers from forcibly collecting debts due their subjects. Germany seemed especially determined to force a settlement of her demands, and it was well known that Germany had for years regarded the Monroe Doctrine as the main hindrance in the way of her acquiring a foothold in Latin America. The only effective method of collecting the interest on the foreign debt of the Dominican Republic appeared to be the seizure and administration of her custom houses by some foreign power or group of foreign powers. President Roosevelt foresaw that such an occupation of the Dominican custom houses would, in view of the large debt, constitute the occupation of American territory by European powers for an indefinite period of time, and would, therefore, be a violation of the Monroe Doctrine. He had before him also the results of a somewhat similar financial administration of Egypt undertaken jointly by England and France in 1878, and after Arabi's revolt continued by England alone, with the result that Egypt soon became a possession of the British crown to almost as great a degree as if it had been formally annexed, and during the World War it was in fact treated as an integral part of the British Empire. President Roosevelt concluded, therefore, that where it was necessary to place a bankrupt American republic in the hands of a receiver, the United States must undertake to act as receiver and take over the administration of its finances. He boldly adopted this policy and finally forced a reluctant Senate to acquiesce. The arrangement has worked admirably. In spite of the criticism that this policy encountered, the Taft administration not only continued it in Santo Domingo, but tried to extend it to Nicaragua and Honduras. In January, 1911, a treaty placing the finances of Honduras under the supervision of the United States was signed by Secretary Knox, and in June a similar treaty was signed with Nicaragua. These treaties provided for the refunding of the foreign debt, in each case through loans made by American bankers and secured by the customs duties, the collector in each case to be approved by the United States and to make an annual report to the Department of State. These treaties were not ratified by the Senate.

Secretary Knox then tried another solution of the question. On February 26, 1913, a new treaty with Nicaragua was submitted to the Senate by the terms of which Nicaragua agreed to give the United States an exclusive right of way for a canal through her territory and a naval base in Fonseca Bay, in return for the payment of three millions of dollars. The Senate failed to act on this treaty, as the close of the Taft administration was then at hand. The Wilson administration followed the same policy, however, and in July, 1913, Mr. Bryan submitted to the Senate a third treaty with Nicaragua containing the provisions of the second Knox treaty and in addition certain provisions of the Platt amendment, which defines our protectorate over Cuba. This treaty aroused strong opposition in the other Central American states, and Costa Rica, Salvador, and Honduras filed formal protests with the United States Government against its ratification on the ground that it would convert Nicaragua into a protectorate of the United States and thus defeat the long-cherished plan for a union of the Central American republics. The Senate of the United States objected to the protectorate feature of the treaty and refused to ratify it, but the negotiations were renewed by the Wilson administration and on February 18, 1916, a new treaty, which omits the provisions of the Platt amendment, was accepted by the Senate. This treaty grants to the United States in perpetuity the exclusive right to construct a canal by way of the San Juan River and Lake Nicaragua, and leases to the United States for ninety-nine years a naval base on the Gulf of Fonseca, and also the Great Corn and Little Corn islands as coaling stations. The consideration for these favors was the sum of three millions of dollars to be expended, with the approval of the Secretary of State of the United States, in paying the public debt of Nicaragua and for other public purposes to be agreed on by the two contracting parties.

The treaty with the black Republic of Haiti, ratified by the Senate February 28, 1916, carries the new Caribbean policies of the United States to the farthest limits short of actual annexation. It provides for the establishment of a receivership of Haitian customs under the control of the United States similar in most respects to that established over the Dominican Republic. It provides further for the appointment, on the nomination of the President of the United States, of a financial adviser, who shall assist in the settlement of the foreign debt and direct expenditures of the surplus for the development of the agricultural, mineral, and commercial resources of the republic. It provides further for a native constabulary under American officers appointed by the President of Haiti upon nomination by the President of the United States. It further extends to

Haiti the main provisions of the Platt amendment. By controlling the internal financial administration of the government the United States hopes to remove all incentives for those revolutions which have in the past had for their object a raid on the public treasury, and by controlling the customs and maintaining order the United States hopes to avoid all possibility of foreign intervention. The treaty is to remain in force for a period of ten years and for another period of ten years if either party presents specific reasons for continuing it on the ground that its purpose has not been fully accomplished.

Prior to the Roosevelt administration the Monroe Doctrine was regarded by the Latin-American states as solely a protective policy. The United States did not undertake to control the financial administration or the foreign policy of any of these republics. It was only after their misconduct had gotten them into difficulty and some foreign power, or group of foreign powers, was on the point of demanding reparation by force that the United States stepped in and undertook to see to it that foreign intervention did not take the form of occupation of territory or interference in internal politics. The Monroe Doctrine has always been in principle a policy of American intervention for the purpose of preventing European intervention, but American intervention always awaited the threat of immediate action on the part of some European power. President Roosevelt concluded that it would be wiser to restrain the reckless conduct of the smaller American republics before disorders or public debts should reach a point which gave European powers an excuse for intervening. In a message to Congress in 1904 he laid down this new doctrine, which soon became famous as the Big Stick policy. He said: "If a nation shows that it knows how to act with reasonable efficiency and decency in social and political matters, if it keeps order and pays its obligations, it need fear no interference from the United States.

Unfortunately President Roosevelt's assertion of the Big Stick policy and of the duty of the United States to play policeman in the western hemisphere was accompanied by his seizure of the Canal Zone. This action naturally aroused serious apprehensions in Latin America and gave color to the charge that the United States had converted the Monroe Doctrine from a protective policy into a policy of selfish aggression. Colombia felt outraged and aggrieved, and this feeling was not alleviated by Mr. Roosevelt's speech several years later to the students of the University of California, in which he boasted of having taken the Canal Zone and said that if he had not taken it as he did, the debate over the matter in Congress would still be going on. Before the close of his administration President Roosevelt undertook to placate Colombia, but the sop which he offered was indignantly rejected. In January, 1909, Secretary Root proposed three treaties, one between the United States and Panama, one between the United States and Colombia, and one between Colombia and Panama. These treaties provided for the recognition of the Republic of Panama by Colombia and for the transference to Colombia of the first ten installments of the annual rental of $250,000 which the United States had agreed to pay to Panama for the lease of the Canal Zone. The treaties were ratified by the United States and by Panama, but not by Colombia.

The Taft administration made repeated efforts to appease Colombia, resulting in the formulation of a definite proposition by Secretary Knox shortly before the close of President Taft's term. His proposals were that if Colombia would ratify the Root treaties just referred to, the United States would be willing to pay $10,000,000 for an exclusive right of way for a canal by the Atrato route and for the perpetual lease of the islands of St. Andrews and Old Providence as coaling stations. These proposals were also rejected. The American minister, Mr. Du Bois, acting, he said, on his own responsibility, then inquired informally whether $25,000,000 without options of any kind would satisfy Colombia. The answer was that Colombia would accept nothing but the arbitration of the whole Panama question. Mr. Knox, in reporting the matter to the President, said that Colombia seemed determined to treat with the incoming Democratic administration. Secretary Bryan took up the negotiations where Knox dropped them, and concluded a treaty, according to the terms of which the United States was to express regret at what had occurred and to pay Colombia $25,000,000. The Senate of the United States refused to ratify this treaty while Wilson was in the White House, but as soon as Harding became president they consented to the payment and ratified the treaty with a few changes in the preamble.

The facts stated above show conclusively that the two most significant developments of American policy in the Caribbean during the last twenty years have been the establishment of formal protectorates and the exercise of financial supervision over weak and disorderly states. Our protectorate over Cuba was clearly defined in the so-called Platt amendment, which was inserted in the army appropriation bill of March 2, 1901, and directed the President to leave control of the island of Cuba to its people so soon as a government should be established under a constitution which defined the future relations with the United States substantially as follows: (1) That the government of Cuba would never enter into any treaty or other compact with any foreign power which would impair the independence of the island; (2) that the said government would not contract any public debt which could not be met by the ordinary revenues of the island; (3) that the government of Cuba would permit the United States to exercise the right to intervene for the preservation of Cuban independence, and for the protection of life, property, and individual liberty; (4) that all acts of the United States in Cuba during its military occupancy thereof should be ratified and validated; (5) that the government of Cuba would carry out the plans already devised for the sanitation of the cities of the island; and finally that the government of Cuba would sell or lease to the United States lands necessary for coaling or naval stations at certain specified points, to be agreed upon with the President of the United States.

It is understood that these articles, with the exception of the fifth, which was proposed by General Leonard Wood, were carefully drafted by Elihu Root, at that time Secretary of War, discussed at length by President McKinley's Cabinet, and entrusted to Senator Platt of Connecticut, who offered them as an amendment to the army appropriation bill. The Wilson administration, as already stated, embodied the first three provisions of the Platt amendment in the Haitian treaty of 1916. Prior to the World War, which has upset all calculations, it seemed highly probable that the Platt amendment would in time be extended to all the weaker states within the zone of the Caribbean. If the United States is to exercise a protectorate over such states, the right to intervene and the conditions of intervention should be clearly defined and publicly proclaimed. Hitherto whatever action we have taken in Latin America has been taken under the Monroe Doctrine—a policy without legal sanction—which an international court might not recognize. Action under a treaty would have the advantage of legality. In other words, the recent treaties with Caribbean states have converted American policy into law.

The charge that in establishing protectorates and financial supervision over independent states we have violated the terms of the Monroe Doctrine is one that has been frequently made. Those who have made it appear to be laboring under the illusion that the Monroe Doctrine was wholly altruistic in its aim. As a matter of fact, the Monroe Doctrine has never been regarded by the United States as in any sense a self-denying declaration. President Monroe said that we should consider any attempt on the part of the European powers "to extend their system to any portion of this hemisphere as dangerous to our peace and safety." The primary object of the policy outlined by President Monroe was, therefore, the peace and safety of the

United States. The protection of Latin-American states against European intervention was merely a means of protecting ourselves. While the United States undertook to prevent the encroachment of European powers in Latin America, it never for one moment admitted any limitation upon the possibility of its own expansion in this region. The whole course of American history establishes the contrary point of view. Since the Monroe Doctrine was enunciated we have annexed at the expense of Latin-American states, Texas, New Mexico, California, and the Canal Zone. Upon other occasions we emphatically declined to bind ourselves by treaty stipulations with England and France that under no circumstance would we annex the island of Cuba. Shortly after the beginning of his first term President Wilson declared in a public address at Mobile that "the United States will never again seek one additional foot of territory by conquest." This declaration introduces a new chapter in American diplomacy.

VIII

THE NEW PAN-AMERICANISM

When President Wilson assumed office March 4, 1913, there was nothing but the Huerta revolution, the full significance of which was not then appreciated, to suggest to his mind the forecast that before the close of his term questions of foreign policy would absorb the attention of the American people and tax to the limit his own powers of mind and body. It seems now a strange fact that neither in his writings nor in his public addresses had President Wilson ever shown any marked interest in questions of international law and diplomacy. He had, on the contrary, made a life-long study of political organization and legislative procedure. Those who knew him had always thought that he was by nature fitted to be a great parliamentary leader and it soon appeared that he had a very definite legislative program which he intended to put through Congress. The foreign problems that confronted him so suddenly and unexpectedly were doubtless felt to be annoying distractions from the work which he had mapped out for himself and which was far more congenial to his tastes. As time went by, however, he was forced to give more and more thought to our relations with Latin America on the one hand and to the European war on the other. His ideas on international problems at first cautiously set forth, soon caught step with the rapid march of events and guided the thought of the world.

The Mexican situation, which reached a crisis a few days before Mr. Wilson came into office, at once demanded his attention and led to the enunciation of a general Latin-American policy. He had scarcely been in office a week when he issued a statement which was forwarded by the secretary of state to all American diplomatic officers in Latin America. In it he said:

"One of the chief objects of my administration will be to cultivate the friendship and deserve the confidence of our sister republics of Central and South America, and to promote in every proper and honorable way the interests which are common to the peoples of the two continents. . . .

"The United States has nothing to seek in Central and South America except the lasting interests of the peoples of the two continents, the security of governments intended for the people and for no special group or interest, and the development of personal and trade relationships between the two continents which shall redound to the profit and advantage of both, and interfere with the rights and liberties of neither.

"From these principles may be read so much of the future policy of this government as it is necessary now to forecast, and in the spirit of these principles I may, I hope, be permitted with as much confidence as earnestness, to extend to the governments of all the republics of America the hand of genuine disinterested friendship and to pledge my own honor and the honor of my colleagues to every enterprise of peace and amity that a fortunate future may disclose."

The policy here outlined, and elaborated a few months later in an address before the Southern Commercial Congress at Mobile, Alabama, has been termed the New Pan-Americanism. The Pan-American ideal is an old one, dating back in fact to the Panama Congress of 1826. The object of this congress was not very definitely stated in the call, which was issued by

Simon Bolivar, but his purpose was to secure the independence and peace of the new Spanish republics through either a permanent confederation or a series of diplomatic congresses. President Adams through Henry Clay, who was at that time Secretary of State, promptly accepted the invitation to send delegates. The matter was debated at such length, however, in the House and Senate that the American delegates did not reach Panama until after the congress had adjourned. In view of the opposition which the whole scheme encountered in Congress, the instructions to the American delegates were very carefully drawn and their powers were strictly limited. They were cautioned against committing their government in any way to the establishment of "an amphictyonic council, invested with power fully to decide controversies between the American states or to regulate in any respect their conduct." They were also to oppose the formation of an offensive and defensive alliance between the American powers, for, as Mr. Clay pointed out, the Holy Alliance had abandoned all idea of assisting Spain in the reconquest of her late colonies. After referring to "the avoidance of foreign alliances as a leading maxim" of our foreign policy, Mr. Clay continued: "Without, therefore, asserting that an exigency may not occur in which an alliance of the most intimate kind between the United States and the other American republics would be highly proper and expedient, it may be safely said that the occasion which would warrant a departure from that established maxim ought to be one of great urgency, and that none such is believed now to exist."

The British Government sent a special envoy to reside near the Congress and to place himself in frank and friendly communication with the delegates. Canning's private instructions to this envoy declared that, "Any project for putting the U. S. of North America at the head of an American Confederacy, as against Europe, would be highly displeasing to your Government. It would be felt as an ill return for the service which has been rendered to those States, and the dangers which have been averted from them, by the countenance and friendship, and public declarations of Great Britain; and it would probably, at no distant period, endanger the peace both of America and of Europe."

The Panama Congress was without practical results and it was more than half a century before the scheme for international coöperation on the part of American states was again taken up. In 1881 Secretary Blaine issued an invitation to the American republics to hold a conference at Washington, but the continuance of the war between Chile and Peru caused an indefinite postponement of the proposed conference. Toward the close of President Cleveland's first administration the invitation was renewed and the First International Conference of American States convened at Washington in 1890. It happened that when the Conference met Mr. Blaine was again Secretary of State and presided over its opening sessions. The most notable achievement of this Conference was the establishment of the Bureau of American Republics, now known as the Pan-American Union. The Second International Conference of American States, held in the City of Mexico in 1901, arranged for all American states to become parties to the Hague Convention of 1899 for the pacific settlement of international disputes and drafted a treaty for the compulsory arbitration, as between American states, of pecuniary claims. The Third Conference, held at Rio Janeiro in 1906, extended the above treaty for another period of five years and proposed that the subject of pecuniary claims be considered at the second Hague Conference. Added significance was given to the Rio Conference by the presence of Secretary Root who, although not a delegate, made it the occasion of a special mission to South America. The series of notable addresses which he delivered on this mission gave a new impetus to the Pan-American movement. The Fourth Conference, held at Buenos Ayres in 1910, was occupied largely with routine matters. It extended the pecuniary claims convention for an indefinite period.

The conferences above referred to were political or diplomatic in character. There have been held two Pan-American Scientific Congresses in which the United States participated, one at Chile in 1908 and one at Washington, December, 1915, to January, 1916. A very important Pan-American Financial Congress was held at Washington in May, 1915. These congresses have accomplished a great deal in the way of promoting friendly feeling as well as the advancement of science and commerce among the republics of the Western Hemisphere.

The American Institute of International Law, organized at Washington in October, 1912, is a body which is likely to have great influence in promoting the peace and welfare of this hemisphere. The Institute is composed of five representatives from the national society of international law in each of the twenty-one American republics. At a session held in the city of Washington, January 6, 1916, the Institute adopted a Declaration of the Rights and Duties of Nations. This declaration, designed to give a solid legal basis to the new Pan-Americanism, was as follows:

I. Every nation has the right to exist and to protect and to conserve its existence; but this right neither implies the right nor justifies the act of the state to protect itself or to conserve its existence by the commission of unlawful acts against innocent and unoffending states.

II. Every nation has the right to independence in the sense that it has a right to the pursuit of happiness and is free to develop itself without interference or control from other states, provided that in so doing it does not interfere with or violate the rights of other states.

III. Every nation is in law and before law the equal of every other nation belonging to the society of nations, and all nations have the right to claim and, according to the Declaration of Independence of the United States, "to assume, among the powers of the earth, the separate and equal station to which the laws of nature and of Nature's God entitle them."

IV. Every nation has the right to territory within defined boundaries, and to exercise exclusive jurisdiction over its territory, and all persons whether native or foreign found therein.

V. Every nation entitled to a right by the law of nations is entitled to have that right respected and protected by all other nations, for right and duty are correlative, and the right of one is the duty of all to observe.

VI. International law is at one and the same time both national and international; national in the sense that it is the law of the land and applicable as such to the decision of all questions involving its principles; international in the sense that it is the law of the society of nations and applicable as such to all questions between and among the members of the society of nations involving its principles.

This Declaration has been criticised as being too altruistic for a world in which diplomacy has been occupied with selfish aims, yet Mr. Root, in presenting it at the annual meeting of the American Society of International Law, claimed that every statement in it was "based upon the decisions of American courts and the authority of American publicists."

The Mexican situation put the principles of the new Pan-Americanism to a severe test. On February 18, 1913, Francisco Madero was seized and imprisoned as the result of a conspiracy formed by one of his generals, Victoriano Huerta, who forthwith proclaimed himself dictator. Four days later Madero was murdered while in the custody of Huerta's troops. Henry Lane Wilson, the American ambassador, promptly urged his government to recognize Huerta, but President Taft, whose term was rapidly drawing to a close, took no action and left the question to his successor.

President Wilson thus had a very disagreeable situation to face when he assumed control of affairs at Washington. He refused to recognize Huerta, whose authority was contested by insurrectionary chiefs in various parts of the country. It was claimed by the critics of the administration that the refusal to recognize Huerta was a direct violation of the well-known American policy of recognizing de facto governments without undertaking to pass upon the rights involved. It is perfectly true that the United States has consistently followed the policy of recognizing de facto governments as soon as it is evident in each case that the new government rests on popular approval and is likely to be permanent. This doctrine of recognition is distinctively an American doctrine. It was first laid down by Thomas Jefferson when he was Secretary of State as an offset to the European doctrine of divine right, and it was the natural outgrowth of that other Jeffersonian doctrine that all governments derive their just powers from the consent of the governed. Huerta could lay no claim to authority derived from a majority or anything like a majority of the Mexican people. He was a self-constituted dictator, whose authority rested solely on military force. President Wilson and Secretary Bryan were fully justified in refusing to recognize his usurpation of power, though they probably made a mistake in announcing that they would never recognize him and in demanding his elimination from the presidential contest. This announcement made him deaf to advice from Washington and utterly indifferent to the destruction of American life and property.

The next step in the President's course with reference to Mexico was the occupation of Vera Cruz. On April 20, 1914, the President asked Congress for authority to employ the armed forces of the United States in demanding redress for the arbitrary arrest of American marines at Vera Cruz, and the next day Admiral Fletcher was ordered to seize the custom house at that port. This he did after a sharp fight with Huerta's troops in which nineteen Americans were killed and seventy wounded. The American chargé d'affaires, Nelson O'Shaughnessy, was at once handed his passports, and all diplomatic relations between the United States and Mexico were severed.

A few days later the representatives of the so-called ABC Alliance, Argentina, Brazil, and Chile, tendered their good offices for a peaceful settlement of the conflict and President Wilson promptly accepted their mediation. The resulting conference at Niagara, May 20, was not successful in its immediate object, but it resulted in the elimination of Huerta who resigned July 15, 1914. On August 20, General Venustiano Carranza, head of one of the revolutionary factions, assumed control of affairs at the capital, but his authority was disputed by General Francisco Villa, another insurrectionary chief. On Carranza's promise to respect the lives and property of American citizens the United States forces were withdrawn from Vera Cruz in November, 1914.

In August, 1915, at the request of President Wilson, the six ranking representatives of Latin America at Washington made an unsuccessful effort to reconcile the contending factions of Mexico. On their advice, however, President Wilson decided in October to recognize the government of Carranza, who now controlled three fourths of the territory of Mexico. As a result of this action Villa began a series of attacks on American citizens and raids across the border, which in March, 1916, compelled the President to send a punitive expedition into Mexico and later to dispatch most of the regular army and large bodies of militia to the border.

The raids of Villa created a very awkward situation. Carranza not only made no real effort to suppress Villa, but he vigorously opposed the steps taken by the United States to protect its own citizens along the border, and even assumed a threatening attitude. There was a loud and persistent demand in the United States for war against Mexico. American investments in land, mines, rubber plantations, and other enterprises were very large, and these financial interests were particularly outraged at the President's policy of "watchful waiting." The President remained deaf to this clamor. No country had been so shamelessly exploited by foreign capital as Mexico. Furthermore, it was suspected and very generally believed that the recent revolutions had been financed by American capital. President Wilson was determined to give the Mexican people an opportunity to reorganize their national life on a better basis and to lend them every assistance in the task. War with Mexico would have been a very serious undertaking and even a successful war would have meant the military occupation of Mexico for an indefinite period. After our entrance into the World War many of those Americans who dissented radically from Wilson's Mexican policy became convinced that his refusal to become involved in war with Mexico was a most fortunate thing for us.

It has been charged that there was a lack of consistency between the President's Mexican policy and his Haitian policy. The difference between the two cases, however, was that order could be restored in Haiti with a relatively small force of marines, while any attempt to apply force to Mexico would have led to a long and bloody conflict. The most novel feature of the President's Mexican policy was his acceptance of the mediation of the ABC Alliance and his subsequent consultation with the leading representatives of Latin America. This action brought the Pan-American ideal almost to the point of realization. It was received with enthusiasm and it placed our relations with Latin America on a better footing than they had been for years.

It was suggested by more than one critic of American foreign policy that if we were to undertake to set the world right, we must come before the bar of public opinion with clean hands, that before we denounced the imperialistic policies of Europe, we should have abandoned imperialistic policies at home. The main features of President Wilson's Latin-American policy, if we may draw a general conclusion, were to pledge American republics not to do anything which would invite European intervention, and to secure by treaty the right of the United States to intervene for the protection of life, liberty, and property, and for the establishment of self-government. Such a policy, unselfishly carried out, was not inconsistent with the general war aims defined by President Wilson.

IX

THE FAILURE OF NEUTRALITY AND ISOLATION

In Washington's day the United States was an experiment in democracy. The vital question was not our duty to the rest of the world, but whether the rest of the world would let us live. The policy of wisdom was to keep aloof from world politics and give as little cause for offense as possible to the great powers of Europe. Washington pointed out that "our detached and distant situation" rendered such a course possible. This policy was justified by events. We were enabled to follow unhindered the bent of our own political genius, to extend our institutions over a vast continent and to attain a position of great prosperity and power in the economic world. While we are still a young country, our government is, with the possible exception of that of Great Britain, the oldest and most stable in the world, and since we declared ourselves a nation and adopted our present constitution the British Government has undergone radical changes of a democratic character. By age and stability we have long been entitled to a voice and influence in the world, and yet we have been singularly indifferent to our responsibilities as a member of the society of nations. We have been in the world, but not of it.

Our policy of isolation corresponded with the situation as it existed a hundred years ago, but not with the situation as it exists to-day and as it has existed for some years past. We no longer occupy a "detached and distant situation." Steam and electricity, the cable and wireless telegraphy have overcome the intervening space and made us the close neighbors of Europe. The whole world has been drawn together in a way that our forefathers never dreamed of, and our commercial, financial, and social relations with the rest of the world are intimate. Under such circumstances political isolation is an impossibility. It has for years been nothing more than a tradition, but a tradition which has tied the hands of American diplomats and caused the American public to ignore what was actually going on in the world. The Spanish War and the acquisition of the Philippines brought us into the full current of world politics, and yet we refused to recognize the changes that inevitably followed.

The emergence of Japan as a first-class power, conscious of achievement and eager to enter on a great career, introduced a new and disturbing element into world politics. Our diplomacy, which had hitherto been comparatively simple, now became exceedingly complex. Formerly the United States was the only great power outside the European balance. The existence of a second detached power greatly complicated the international situation and presented opportunities for new combinations. We have already seen how Germany undertook to use the opportunity presented by Russia's war with Japan to humiliate France and that the United States took a prominent part in the Algeciras Conference for the purpose of preventing the threatened overthrow of the European balance of power. Thus, even before the World War began, it had become evident to close observers of international affairs that the European balance would soon be superseded by a world balance in which the United States would be forced to take its place.

It took a world war, however, to dispel the popular illusion of isolation and to arouse us to a temporary sense of our international responsibilities. When the war began the President, following the traditions of a hundred years, issued, as a matter of course, a proclamation of neutrality, and he thought that the more scrupulously it was observed the greater would be the opportunity for the United States to act as impartial mediator in the final adjustment of peace terms. As the fierceness of the conflict grew it became evident that the role of neutral would not be an easy one to play and that the vital interests of the United States would be involved to a far greater extent than anyone had foreseen.

Neutrality in the modern sense is essentially an American doctrine and the result of our policy of isolation. If we were to keep out of European conflicts, it was necessary for us to pursue a course of rigid impartiality in wars between European powers. In the Napoleonic wars we insisted that neutrals had certain rights which belligerents were bound to respect and we fought the War of 1812 with England in order to establish that principle. Half a century later, in the American Civil War, we insisted that neutrals had certain duties which every belligerent had a right to expect them to perform, and we forced Great Britain in the settlement of the *Alabama* Claims to pay us damages to the extent of $15,500,000 for having failed to perform her neutral obligations. We have thus been the leading champion of the rights and duties of neutrals, and the principles for which we have contended have been written into the modern law of nations. When two or three nations are engaged in war and the rest of the world is neutral, there is usually very little difficulty in enforcing neutral rights, but when a majority of the great powers are at war, it is impossible for the remaining great powers, much less for the smaller neutrals, to maintain their rights. This was true in the Napoleonic wars, but at that time the law of neutrality was in its infancy and had never been fully recognized by the powers at war. The failure of neutrality in the Great War was far more serious, for the rights of neutrals had been clearly defined and universally recognized.

Notwithstanding the large German population in this country and the propaganda which we now know that the German Government had systematically carried on for years in our very midst, the invasion of Belgium and the atrocities committed by the Germans soon arrayed opinion on the side of the Allies. This was not a departure from neutrality, for it should be remembered that neutrality is not an attitude of mind, but a legal status. As long as our Government fulfilled its obligations as defined by the law of nations, no charge of a violation of neutrality could be justly made. To deny to the citizens of a neutral country the right to express their moral judgments would be to deny that the world can ever be governed by public opinion. The effort of the German propagandists to draw a distinction between so-called ethical and legal neutrality was plausible, but without real force. While neutrality is based on the general principle of impartiality, this principle has been embodied in a fairly well-defined set of rules which may, and frequently do, in any given war, work to the advantage of one belligerent and to the disadvantage of the other. In the Great War this result was brought about by the naval superiority of Great Britain. So far as our legal obligations to Germany were concerned she had no cause for complaint. If, on the other hand, our conduct had been determined solely by ethical considerations, we would have joined the Allies long before we did.

The naval superiority of Great Britain made it comparatively easy for her to stop all direct trade with the enemy in articles contraband of war, but this was of little avail so long as Germany could import these articles through the neutral ports of Italy, Holland, and the Scandinavian countries. Under these circumstances an ordinary blockade of the German coast would have had little effect. Therefore, no such blockade was proclaimed by Great Britain. She adopted other methods of cutting off overseas supplies from Germany. She enlarged the lists of both absolute and conditional contraband and under the doctrine of continuous voyage seized articles on both lists bound for Germany through neutral countries.

As to the right of a belligerent to enlarge the contraband lists there can be no doubt. Even the Declaration of London, which undertook for the first time to establish an international classification of contraband, provided in Article 23 that "articles and materials which are exclusively used for war may be added to the list of absolute contraband by means of a notified declaration," and Article 25 provided that the list of conditional contraband might be enlarged in the same manner. Under modern conditions of warfare it would seem impossible to determine in advance what articles are to be treated as contraband. During the Great War many articles regarded in previous wars as innocent became indispensable to the carrying on of the war.

Great Britain's application of the doctrine of continuous voyage was more open to dispute. She assumed that contraband articles shipped to neutral countries adjacent to Germany and Austria were intended for them unless proof to the contrary was forthcoming, and she failed to draw any distinction between absolute and conditional contraband. The United States protested vigorously against this policy, but the force of its protest was weakened by the fact that during the Civil War the American Government had pursued substantially the same policy in regard to goods shipped by neutrals to Nassau, Havana, Matamoros, and other ports adjacent to the Confederacy. Prior to the American Civil War goods could not be seized on any grounds unless bound directly for a belligerent port. Under the English doctrine of continuous voyage as advanced during the Napoleonic wars, goods brought from the French West Indies to the United States and reshipped to continental Europe were condemned by the British Admiralty Court on the ground that notwithstanding the unloading and reloading at an American port the voyage from the West Indies to Europe was in effect a continuous voyage, and under the Rule of 1756 Great Britain refused to admit the right of neutral ships to engage in commerce between France and her colonies. Great Britain, however, seized ships only on the second leg of the voyage, that is, when bound directly for a belligerent port. During the American Civil War the United States seized goods under an extension of the English doctrine on the first leg of the voyage, that is, while they were in transit from one neutral port to another neutral port, on the ground that they were to be subsequently shipped in another vessel to a Confederate port. Great Britain adopted and applied the American doctrine during the Boer War. The doctrine of continuous voyage, as applied by the United States and England, was strongly condemned by most of the continental writers on international law. The Declaration of London adopted a compromise by providing that absolute contraband might be seized when bound through third countries, but that conditional contraband was not liable to capture under such circumstances. As the Declaration of London was not ratified by the British Government this distinction was ignored, and conditional as well as absolute contraband was seized when bound for Germany through neutral countries.

While Great Britain may be charged with having unwarrantably extended the application of certain rules of international law and may have rendered herself liable to pecuniary damages, she displayed in all her measures a scrupulous regard for human life. Her declaration that "The whole of the North Sea must be considered a military area," was explained as an act of retaliation against Germany for having scattered floating mines on the high seas in the path of British commerce. She did not undertake to exclude neutral vessels from the North Sea, but merely notified them that certain areas had been mined and warned them not to enter without receiving sailing directions from the British squadron.

The German decree of February 4, 1915, establishing a submarine blockade or "war zone" around the British Isles, on the other hand, was absolutely without legal justification. It did not fulfill the requirements of a valid blockade, because it cut off only a very small percentage of British commerce, and the first requirement of a blockade is that it must be effective. The decree was aimed directly at enemy merchant vessels and indirectly at the ships of neutrals. It utterly ignored the well-recognized right of neutral passengers to travel on merchant vessels of belligerents. The second decree announcing unrestricted submarine warfare after February 1, 1917, was directed against neutral as well as enemy ships. It undertook to exclude all neutral ships from a wide zone extending far out on the high seas, irrespective of their mission or the character of their cargo. It was an utter defiance of all law.

The citizens of neutral countries have always had the right to travel on the merchant vessels of belligerents, subject, of course, to the risk of capture and detention. The act of the German ambassador in inserting an advertisement in a New York paper warning Americans not to take passage on the *Lusitania*, when the President had publicly asserted that they had a perfect right to travel on belligerent ships, was an insolent and unparalleled violation of diplomatic usage and would have justified his instant dismissal. Some action would probably have been taken by the State Department had not the incident been overshadowed by the carrying out of the threat and the actual destruction of the *Lusitania*.

The destruction of enemy prizes at sea is recognized by international law under exceptional circumstances and subject to certain definite restrictions, but an unlimited right of destruction even of enemy merchant vessels had never been claimed by any authority on international law or by any government prior to the German decree. The destruction of neutral prizes, though practised by some governments, has not been so generally acquiesced in, and when resorted to has been attended by an even more rigid observance of the rules designed to safeguard human life. Article 48 of the Declaration of London provided that, "A captured neutral vessel is not to be destroyed by the captor, but must be taken into such port as is proper in order to determine there the rights as regards the validity of the capture." Unfortunately Article 49 largely negatived this statement by leaving the whole matter to the discretion of the captor. It is as follows: "As an exception, a neutral vessel captured by a belligerent ship, and which would be liable to condemnation, may be destroyed if the observance of Article 48 would involve danger to the ship of war or to the success of the operations in which she is at the time engaged." The next article provided the following safeguards: "Before the destruction the persons on board must be placed in safety, and all the ship's papers and other documents which those interested consider relevant for the decision as to the validity of the capture must be taken on board the ship of war."

The Declaration of London was freely criticised for recognizing an unlimited discretionary right on the part of a captor to destroy a neutral prize. Under all the circumstances the main grievance against Germany was not that she destroyed prizes at sea, but that she utterly ignored the restrictions imposed upon this right and the rules designed to safeguard human life.

Germany sought to justify her submarine policy on the ground (1) that the American manufacture and sale of munitions of war was one-sided and therefore unneutral, and (2) that the United States had practically acquiesced in what she considered the unlawful efforts of Great Britain to cut off the food supply of Germany. The subject of the munitions trade was brought to the attention of the United States by Germany in a note of April 4, 1915. While not denying the legality of the trade in munitions under ordinary circumstances the contentions of the German Government were that the situation in the present war differed from that of any previous war; that the recognition of the trade in the past had sprung from the necessity of protecting existing industries, while in the present war an entirely new industry had been created in the United States; and it concluded with the following statement which was the real point of the note: "This industry is actually delivering goods to the enemies of Germany. The theoretical willingness to supply Germany also, if shipments were possible, does not alter the case. If it is the will of the American people that there should be a true neutrality, the United States will find means of preventing this one-sided supply of arms or at least of utilizing it to protect legitimate trade with Germany, especially that in food stuffs." To this note Secretary Bryan replied that "Any change in its own laws of neutrality during the progress of the war which would affect unequally the relations of the United States with the nations at war would be an unjustifiable departure from the principle of strict neutrality."

Two months later the discussion was renewed by the Austro-Hungarian Government. The Austrian note did not question the intention of the United States to conform to the letter of the law, but complained that we were not carrying out its spirit, and suggested that a threat to withhold food stuffs and raw materials from the Allies would be sufficient to protect legitimate commerce between the United States and the Central Powers. To this note Secretary Lansing replied at length. He held: (1) that the United States was under no obligation to change or modify the rules of international usage on account of special conditions. (2) He rejected what he construed to be the contention of the Austrian Government that "the advantages gained to a belligerent by its superiority on the sea should be equalized by the neutral powers by the establishment of a system of non-intercourse with the victor." (3) He called attention to the fact that Austria-Hungary and Germany had during the years preceding the present European war produced "a great surplus of arms and ammunition which they sold throughout the world and especially to belligerents. Never during that period did either of them suggest or apply the principle now advocated by the Imperial and Royal Government." (4) "But, in addition to the question of principle, there is a practical and substantial reason why the Government of the United States has from the foundation of the Republic to the present time advocated and practised unrestricted trade in arms and military supplies. It has never been the policy of this country to maintain in time of peace a large military establishment or stores of arms and ammunition sufficient to repel invasion by a well-equipped and powerful enemy. It has desired to remain at peace with all nations and to avoid any appearance of menacing such peace by the threat of its armies and navies. In consequence of this standing policy the United States would, in the event of attack by a foreign power, be at the outset of the war seriously, if not fatally, embarrassed by the lack of arms and ammunition and by the means to produce them in sufficient quantities to supply the requirements of national defense. The United States has always depended upon the right and power to purchase arms and ammunition from neutral nations in case of foreign attack. This right, which it claims for itself, it cannot deny to others."

The German and Austrian authorities were fully aware that their arguments had no basis in international law or practice. Indeed, their notes were probably designed to influence public opinion and help the German propagandists in this country who were making a desperate effort to get Congress to place an embargo on the export of munitions. Having failed in this attempt, an extensive conspiracy was formed to break up the trade in munitions by a resort to criminal methods. Numerous explosions occurred in munition plants destroying many lives and millions of dollars' worth of property, and bombs were placed in a number of ships engaged in carrying supplies to the Allies. The Austrian ambassador and the German military and naval attachés at Washington were involved in these activities and their recall was promptly demanded by Secretary Lansing.

The violations of international law by Germany were so flagrant, her methods of waging war so barbarous, the activities of her diplomats so devoid of honor, and her solemn pledges were so ruthlessly broken that the technical discussion of the rules of maritime law was completely overshadowed by the higher moral issues involved in the contest. All further efforts to maintain neutrality finally became intolerable even to President Wilson, who had exercised patience until patience ceased to be a virtue. Having failed in his efforts to persuade Congress to authorize the arming of merchantmen, the President finally concluded, in view of Germany's threat to treat armed guards as pirates, that armed neutrality was impracticable. He accepted the only alternative and on April 2, 1917, went before Congress to ask for a formal declaration of war against Germany.

Had Germany observed the rules of international law, the United States would probably have remained neutral notwithstanding the imminent danger of the overthrow of France and the possible invasion of England. The upsetting of the European balance would eventually have led to a conflict between Germany and the United States. The violation of American rights forced us to go to war, but having once entered the war, we fought not merely for the vindication of American rights, but for the establishment of human freedom and the recognition of human rights throughout the world. In his war address President Wilson said: "Neutrality is no longer feasible or desirable where the peace of the world is involved and the freedom of its peoples, and the menace to that peace and freedom lies in the existence of autocratic Governments backed by organized force which is controlled wholly by their will, not by the will of their people. We have seen the last of neutrality in such circumstances." Having once abandoned neutrality and isolation we are not likely to remain neutral again in any war which involves the balance of power in the world or the destinies of the major portion of mankind. Neutrality and isolation were correlative. They were both based on the view that we were a remote and distant people and had no intimate concern with what was going on in the great world across the seas.

The failure of neutrality and the abandonment of isolation marked a radical, though inevitable, change in our attitude toward world politics. President Wilson did not propose, however, to abandon the great principles for which we as a nation had stood, but rather to extend them and give them a world-wide application. In his address to the Senate on January 22, 1917, he said:

"I am proposing, as it were, that the nations should with one accord adopt the doctrine of President Monroe as the doctrine of the world; that no nation should seek to extend its polity over any other nation or people, but that every people should be left free to determine its own polity, its own way of development, unhindered, unthreatened, unafraid, the little along with the great and powerful.

"I am proposing that all nations henceforth avoid entangling alliances which would draw them into competitions of power, catch them in a net of intrigue and selfish rivalry, and disturb their own affairs with influences intruded from without. There is no entangling alliance in a concert of power."

In other words, the Monroe Doctrine, stripped of its imperialistic tendencies, was to be internationalized, and the American policy of isolation, in the sense of avoiding secret alliances, was to become a fundamental principle of the new international order. If the United States was to go into a league of nations, every member of the league must stand on its own footing. We were not to be made a buffer between alliances and ententes.

X

THE WAR AIMS OF THE UNITED STATES

The advent of the United States into the family of nations nearly a century and a half ago was an event of worldwide significance. Our revolutionary ancestors set up a government founded on a new principle, happily phrased by Jefferson in the statement that governments derive their just powers from the consent of the governed. This principle threatened, although remotely, the existence of the aristocratic governments of the Old World which were still based on the doctrine of divine right. The entrance of the United States into the World War was an event of equal significance because it gave an American president, who was thoroughly grounded in the political philosophy of the Virginia Bill of Rights, the Declaration of Independence, and the writings of the founders of the Republic, an opportunity to proclaim to the world the things for which America has always stood. In this connection H. W. V. Temperley in "A History of the Peace Conference of Paris" (vol. i, page 173) says: "The utterances of President Wilson have a unique significance, not only because they were taken as the legal basis of the Peace negotiations, but because they form a definite and coherent body of political doctrine. This doctrine, though developed and expanded in view of the tremendous changes produced by the war, was not formed or even altered by them. His ideas, like those of no other great statesman of the war, are capable of being worked out as a complete political philosophy. A peculiar interest, therefore, attaches to his pre-war speeches, for they contain the germs of his political faith and were not influenced by the terrifying portents of to-day. The tenets in themselves were few and simple, but their consequences, when developed by the war, were such as to produce the most far-reaching results. It is not possible or necessary to discuss how far these tenets were accepted by the American people as a whole, for, as the utterances of their legal representative at a supreme moment of world history, they will always retain their value."

The principal features of Wilson's political philosophy were revealed in his policy toward Latin America before he had any idea of intervening in the European situation. At the outset of his administration he declared that the United States would "never again seek one additional foot of territory by conquest." In December, 1915, he declared: "From the first we have made common cause with all partisans of liberty on this side of the sea and . . . have set America aside as a whole for the uses of independent nations and political freemen." A few weeks later he proposed that the nations of America should unite "in guaranteeing to each other absolute political independence and territorial integrity." This proposal was actually embodied in a treaty, but this plan for an American league of nations did not meet with the approval of the other states, who probably feared that the United States would occupy too dominant a position in such a league. President Wilson's refusal to recognize the despotic power of Huerta, while expressing sympathy for the people of Mexico, was the first application of the policy which later so successfully drove a wedge in between the Kaiser and the German people. His refusal to invade Mexico and his determination to give the people of that country a chance to work out their own salvation gave evidence to the world of the unselfishness and sincerity of his policies, and paved the way for the moral leadership which he later exercised over the peoples of Europe.

President Wilson's insistence on neutrality in "thought, word, and deed," the expression "too proud to fight," and his statement in regard to the war, May 27, 1916, that "with its causes and objects we are not concerned," caused deep offense to many of his countrymen and were received with ridicule by others at home and abroad. His reasons for remaining neutral were best stated in the speech accepting his second nomination for the presidency, September 2, 1916: "We have been neutral not only because it was the fixed and traditional policy of the United States to stand aloof from the politics of Europe and because we had had no part either of action or of policy in the influences which brought on the present war, but also because it was manifestly our duty to prevent, if it were possible, the indefinite extension of the fires of hate and desolation kindled by that terrible conflict and seek to serve mankind by reserving our strength and our resources for the anxious and difficult days of restoration and healing which must follow, when peace will have to build its house anew."

Other speeches made during the year 1916 show, however, that he was being gradually forced to the conclusion that "peace is not always within the choice of the nation" and that we must be "ready to fight for our rights when those rights are coincident with the rights of man and humanity."

After the German peace proposals of December 12, 1916, President Wilson called on all the belligerents to state publicly what they were fighting for. This demand caused a searching of hearts everywhere, led to a restatement of aims on the part of the Allies, and threw the Central Governments on the defensive. In formulating their replies the Allies were somewhat embarrassed by the secret treaties relating to Russia and Italy, which were later made public by the Bolsheviki. In March, 1915, England and France had made an agreement with Russia by which she was to get Constantinople, the aim of her policy since the days of Peter the Great. By the secret Treaty of London, signed April 26, 1915, England, France, and

Russia had promised Italy that she should receive the Trentino and Southern Tyrol, including in its population more than 250,000 Germans. Italy was also promised Trieste and the Istrian peninsula, the boundary running just west of Fiume, over which city, it should be remembered, she acquired no claim under this treaty. Italy was also to receive about half of Dalmatia, including towns over half of whose population were Jugo-Slavs. To President Wilson's note the Allies had to reply, therefore, in somewhat general terms. Their territorial demands were: "The restitution of provinces formerly torn from the Allies by force or against the wish of their inhabitants; the liberation of the Italians, as also of the Slavs, Roumanes, and Czecho-Slovaks from foreign domination, the setting free of the populations subject to the bloody tyranny of the Turks; and the turning out of Europe of the Ottoman Empire as decidedly foreign to Western civilization." The German reply contained no statement of territorial claims and gave no pledge even as to the future status of Belgium.

In reporting the results of this interchange of views to the Senate, January 22, 1917, President Wilson delivered the first of that series of addresses on the essentials of a just and lasting peace which made him the recognized spokesman of the liberal element in all countries and gained for him a moral leadership that was without parallel in the history of the world. "In every discussion of the peace that must end this war," he declared, "it is taken for granted that that peace must be followed by some definite concert of power which will make it virtually impossible that any such catastrophe should ever overwhelm us again. Every lover of mankind, every sane and thoughtful man must take that for granted." In fact, there was no dissent from this statement. Most of our leading men, including Taft, Roosevelt, and Lodge, were committed to the idea of a league of nations for the maintenance of law and international peace. The League to Enforce Peace, which had branches in all the Allied countries, had done a great work in popularizing this idea. The President came before the Senate, he said, "as the council associated with me in the final determination of our international obligations," to formulate the conditions upon which he would feel justified in asking the American people to give "formal and solemn adherence to a League for Peace." He disclaimed any right to a voice in determining what the terms of peace should be, but he did claim a right to "have a voice in determining whether they shall be made lasting or not by the guarantees of a universal covenant." First of all, the peace must be a "peace without victory," for "only a peace between equals can last." And, he added, "there is a deeper thing involved than even equality of right among organized nations. No peace can last, or ought to last, which does not recognize and accept the principle that governments derive all their just powers from the consent of the governed, and that no right anywhere exists to hand peoples about from sovereignty to sovereignty as if they were property." He cited Poland as an example, declaring that statesmen everywhere were agreed that she should be "united, independent, and autonomous."

He declared that every great people "should be assured a direct outlet to the sea," and that "no nation should be shut away from free access to the open paths of the world's commerce." He added: "The freedom of the seas is the *sine qua non* of peace, equality, and coöperation." This problem, he said, was closely connected with the limitation of naval armaments. "The question of armaments, whether on land or sea, is the most immediately and intensely practical question connected with the future fortunes of nations and of mankind."

The Russian revolution, which came in March, 1917, and resulted in the overthrow of the Czar's government, cleared the political atmosphere for the time being, and enabled President Wilson in his address to Congress on April 2 to proclaim a war of democracy against autocracy. The new Russian government repudiated all imperialistic aims and adopted the formula:

"Self-determination, no annexations, no indemnities." Poland was given her freedom and the demand for Constantinople was abandoned. The Allies were thus relieved from one of their most embarrassing secret treaties.

Even after America entered the war, President Wilson continued to advance the same ideas as to the ultimate conditions of peace. His attitude remained essentially different from that of the Allies, who were hampered by secret treaties wholly at variance with the President's aims. In his war address he declared that we had "no quarrel with the German people. We have no feeling towards them but one of sympathy and friendship. It was not upon their impulse that their government acted in entering this war." Prussian autocracy was the object of his attack. "We are now about to accept gauge of battle with this natural foe to liberty and shall, if necessary, spend the whole force of the nation to check and nullify its pretensions and its power. We are glad, now that we see the facts with no veil of false pretense about them, to fight thus for the ultimate peace of the world and for the liberation of its peoples, the German peoples included: for the rights of nations great and small and the privilege of men everywhere to choose their way of life and of obedience. The world must be made safe for democracy. Its peace must be planted upon the tested foundations of political liberty. We have no selfish ends to serve. We desire no conquest, no dominion. We seek no indemnities for ourselves, no material compensation for the sacrifices we shall freely make. We are but one of the champions of the rights of mankind. We shall be satisfied when those rights have been made as secure as the faith and the freedom of nations can make them."

About the time that the United States declared war, Austria and Germany began another so-called "peace offensive." Overtures were made by Austria to France in March, and in August the Pope made a direct appeal to the Powers. This move was unmasked by President Wilson in a public address at the Washington Monument, June 14, 1917. "The military masters under whom Germany is bleeding," he declared, "see very clearly to what point fate has brought them: if they fall back or are forced back an inch, their power abroad and at home will fall to pieces. It is their power at home of which they are thinking now more than of their power abroad. It is that power which is trembling under their very feet. Deep fear has entered their hearts. They have but one chance to perpetuate their military power, or even their controlling political influence. If they can secure peace now, with the immense advantage still in their hands, they will have justified themselves before the German people. They will have gained by force what they promised to gain by it—an immense expansion of German power and an immense enlargement of German industrial and commercial opportunities. Their prestige will be secure, and with their prestige their political power. If they fail, their people will thrust them aside. A government accountable to the people themselves will be set up in Germany, as has been the case in England, the United States, and France—in all great countries of modern times except Germany. If they succeed they are safe, and Germany and the world are undone. If they fail, Germany is saved and the world will be at peace. If they succeed, America will fall within the menace, and we, and all the rest of the world, must remain armed, as they will remain, and must make ready for the next step in their aggression. If they fail, the world may unite for peace and Germany may be of the union."

The task of replying to the Pope was left by the Allied governments to Wilson, who was not hampered by secret treaties. In this remarkable document he drove still further the wedge between the German people and the Kaiser. "The American people have suffered intolerable wrongs at the hands of the Imperial German Government, but they desire no reprisal upon the German people who have themselves suffered all things in this war which they did not choose. They believe that peace should rest upon the rights of peoples, not the rights of Governments—the rights of peoples great or small, weak or powerful—their equal right to freedom and security and self-government and to a participation upon fair terms in the economic opportunities of the world, the German people of course included if they will accept equality and not seek domination."

In conclusion he said: "We cannot take the word of the present rulers of Germany as a guarantee of anything that is to endure, unless explicitly supported by such conclusive evidence of the will and purpose of the German people themselves as the other peoples of the world would be justified in accepting. Without such guarantees, treaties of settlement, agreements for disarmament, covenants to set up arbitration in the place of force, territorial adjustments, reconstitutions of small nations, if made with the German Government, no man, no nation could now depend on. We must await some new evidence of the purposes of the great peoples of the Central Powers. God grant it may be given soon and in a way to restore the confidence of all peoples everywhere in the faith of nations and the possibility of covenanted peace."

Early in November, 1917, the Kerensky Government was overthrown in Russia and the Bolsheviki came into power. They at once proposed a general armistice and called upon all the belligerents to enter into peace negotiations. The Central Powers accepted the invitation, and early in December negotiations began at Brest-Litovsk. The Russian peace proposals were: the evacuation of occupied territories, self-determination for nationalities not hitherto independent, no war indemnities or economic boycotts, and the settlement of colonial questions in accordance with the above principles. The Austrian minister, Count Czernin, replied for the Central Powers, accepting more of the Russian program than had been expected, but rejecting the principle of a free plebiscite for national groups not hitherto independent, and conditioning the whole on the acceptance by the Allies of the offer of general peace. The conference called on the Allies for an answer by January 4. No direct reply was made to this demand, but the Russian proposals had made a profound impression on the laboring classes in all countries, and both Lloyd George and President Wilson felt called on to define more clearly the war aims of the Allies.

In a speech delivered January 5, 1918, Lloyd George made the first comprehensive and authoritative statement of British war aims. He had consulted the labor leaders and Viscount Grey and Mr. Asquith, as well as some of the representatives of the overseas dominions, and he was speaking, he said, for "the nation and the Empire as a whole." He explained first what the British were not fighting for. He disclaimed any idea of overthrowing the German Government, although he considered military autocracy "a dangerous anachronism"; they were not fighting to destroy Austria-Hungary, but genuine self-government must be granted to "those Austro-Hungarian nationalities who have long desired it"; they were not fighting "to deprive Turkey of its capital or of the rich and renowned lands of Thrace, which are predominantly Turkish in race," but the passage between the Mediterranean and the Black Sea must be "internationalized and neutralized." The positive statement of aims included the complete restoration of Belgium, the return of Alsace-Lorraine to France, rectification of the Italian boundary, the independence of Poland, the restoration of Serbia, Montenegro, and the occupied parts of France, Italy, and Rumania, and a disposition of the German colonies with "primary regard to the wishes and interests of the native inhabitants of such colonies." He insisted on reparation for injuries done in violation of international law, but disclaimed a demand for war indemnity. In conclusion he declared the following conditions to be essential to a lasting peace: "First, the sanctity of treaties must be reëstablished; secondly, a territorial settlement must be secured, based on the right of self-determination or the consent of the governed; and lastly, we must seek, by the creation of some international organization, to limit the burden of armaments and diminish the probability of war."

On January 8, 1918, three days after Lloyd George's speech, President Wilson appeared before both Houses of Congress and delivered the most important of all his addresses on war aims. It contained the famous Fourteen Points:

I. Open covenants of peace, openly arrived at, after which there shall be no private international understandings of any kind, but diplomacy shall proceed always frankly and in the public view.

II. Absolute freedom of navigation upon the seas, outside territorial waters, alike in peace and in war, except as the seas may be closed in whole or in part by international action for the enforcement of international covenants.

III. The removal, so far as possible, of all economic barriers and the establishment of an equality of trade conditions among all the nations consenting to the peace and associating themselves for its maintenance.

IV. Adequate guarantees given and taken that national armaments will be reduced to the lowest point consistent with domestic safety.

V. A free, open-minded and absolutely impartial adjustment of all colonial claims, based upon a strict observance of the principle that in determining all such questions of sovereignty the interests of the populations concerned must have equal weight with the equitable claims of the Government whose title is to be determined.

VI. The evacuation of all Russian territory and such a settlement of all questions affecting Russia as will secure the best and freest coöperation of the other nations of the world in obtaining for her an unhampered and unembarrassed opportunity for the independent determination of her own political development and national policy and assure her of a sincere welcome into the society of free nations under institutions of her own choosing; and, more than a welcome, assistance also of every kind that she may need and may herself desire. The treatment accorded Russia by her sister nations will be the acid test of their good will, of their comprehension of her needs as distinguished from their own interests and of their intelligent and unselfish sympathy.

VII. Belgium, the whole world will agree, must be evacuated and restored, without any attempt to limit the sovereignty which she enjoys in common with all other free nations. No other single act will serve as this will serve to restore confidence among the nations in the laws which they have themselves set and determined for the government of their relations with one another. Without this healing act the whole structure and validity of international law is forever impaired.

VIII. All French territory should be freed and the invaded portions restored, and the wrong done to France by Prussia in 1871 in the matter of Alsace-Lorraine, which has unsettled the peace of the world for nearly fifty years, should be righted, in order that peace may once more be made secure in the interest of all.

IX. A readjustment of the frontiers of Italy should be effected along clearly recognizable lines of nationality.

X. The peoples of Austria-Hungary, whose place among the nations we wish to see safeguarded and assured, should be accorded the freest opportunity of autonomous development.

XI. Rumania, Serbia, and Montenegro should be evacuated: occupied territories restored; Serbia accorded free and secure access to the sea; and the relations of the several Balkan states to one another determined by friendly counsel along historically established lines of allegiance and nationality; and international guarantees of the political and economic independence and territorial integrity of the several Balkan states should be entered into.

XII. The Turkish portions of the present Ottoman Empire should be assured a secure sovereignty, but the other nationalities which are now under Turkish rule should be assured an undoubted security of life and an absolutely unmolested opportunity of autonomous development, and the Dardanelles should be permanently opened as a free passage to the ships and commerce of all nations under international guarantees.

XIII. An independent Polish state should be erected which should include the territories inhabited by indisputably Polish populations, which should be assured a free and secure access to the sea, and whose political and economic independence and territorial integrity should be guaranteed by international covenant.

XIV. A general association of nations must be formed under specific covenants for the purpose of affording mutual guarantees of political independence and territorial integrity to great and small states alike.

In February negotiations at Brest-Litovsk were broken off as a result of the excessive demands of the Germans and the armistice was declared at an end. The Germans quickly overran Poland and the Baltic provinces and occupied Ukraine under a treaty which virtually placed the material resources of that country at the disposal of the Central Powers. In an address at Baltimore, April 6, the anniversary of our entrance into the war, President Wilson denounced the insincerity and perfidy of the German rulers, who, he said, were "enjoying in Russia a cheap triumph in which no

In reply the President asked for a clearer understanding on three points: (1) Did the Imperial Chancellor mean that the German Government accepted the terms laid down in the President's addresses referred to, and "that its object in entering into discussion would be only to agree upon the practical details of their application?" (2) The President would not feel at liberty to propose a cessation of arms to the Allied Governments so long as the armies of the Central Powers were upon their soil. (3) The President asked whether the Chancellor was speaking for the constituted authorities of the Empire who had so far conducted the war.

The German reply of October 12 was satisfactory on the first point. With respect to the withdrawal of their troops from occupied territory they proposed a mixed commission to arrange the details. On the third point it was stated that the new government had been formed in agreement with the great majority of the Reichstag. Having accomplished this much, the President's next step was skilfully taken. He replied that the process of evacuation and the conditions of an armistice were matters which must be left to the judgment of the military advisers of the United States and the Allied Governments, but that he would not agree to any arrangement which did not provide "absolutely satisfactory safeguards and guarantees of the maintenance of the present military supremacy of the armies of the United States and of the Allies in the field." Referring next to submarine warfare, he declared that the United States and the Allied Governments could not consider an armistice "so long as the armed forces of Germany continue the illegal and inhumane practices which they persist in." In conclusion he referred to a clause contained in his speech of July 4, now accepted by the German Government as one of the conditions of peace, namely, "The destruction of every arbitrary power anywhere that can separately, secretly, and of its single choice disturb the peace of the world." He added: "The power which has hitherto controlled the German nation is of the sort here described. It is within the choice of the German nation to alter it." He demanded that the United States and the Allied Governments "should know beyond a peradventure" with whom they were dealing.

In reply the Chancellor assured the President that a bill had been introduced in the Reichstag to alter the constitution of the Empire so as to give the representatives of the people the right to decide for war or peace, but the President was not satisfied that there had been any real change. "It may be that future wars have been brought under the control of the German people, but the present war has not been; and it is with the present war that we are dealing." He was not willing to accept any armistice which did not make a renewal of hostilities on the part of Germany impossible. If, he concluded, the United States "must deal with the military masters and the monarchical autocrats of Germany now, or if it is likely to have to deal with them later in regard to the international obligations of the German Empire, it must demand not peace negotiations but surrender. Nothing can be gained by leaving this essential thing unsaid." This note was written October 23. Four days later the Chancellor replied: "The President knows the deep-rooted changes which have taken place and are still taking place in German constitutional life. The peace negotiations will be conducted by a People's Government, in whose hands the decisive legal power rests in accordance with the Constitution, and to which the Military Power will also be subject. The German Government now awaits the proposals for an armistice which will introduce a peace of justice such as the President in his manifestations has described."

The terms of the Armistice were drawn up by the Interallied Council at Versailles and completed by November 5. They were much more severe than the public had expected them to be. Germany was required immediately to evacuate Belgium, France, Alsace-Lorraine, and Luxemburg; to withdraw her armies from the entire territory on the left bank of the Rhine, and from Russia, Austria-Hungary, Rumania, and Turkey; she was to surrender enormous quantities of heavy artillery and airplanes, all her submarines, and most of her battleships, cruisers, and destroyers. This was practically unconditional surrender. Contrary to the general belief at the time, it is now known that Foch and Haig considered these terms too severe and feared that Germany would not accept them. They wanted an armistice that Germany would accept. General Bliss, on the other hand, wanted to demand "the complete disarmament and demobilization of the military and naval forces of the enemy." In America there was much criticism of the President for being willing to negotiate with Germany at all. "On to Berlin" was a popular cry, and it was thought that the President was preventing a complete military triumph. On October 10 Senator Lodge declared in the Senate: "The Republican party stands for unconditional surrender and complete victory, just as Grant stood. My own belief is that the American people mean to have an unconditional surrender. They mean to have a dictated, not a negotiated peace."

After reviewing the Armistice negotiations André Tardieu, a member of the French Cabinet and delegate to the Peace Conference, says:

"What remains of the fiction, believed by so many, of an armistice secretly determined upon by an American dictator; submitted to by the European governments: imposed by their weakness upon the victorious armies, despite the opposition of the generals? The Armistice was discussed in the open light of day. President Wilson only consented to communicate it to his associates on the triple condition that its principle be approved by the military authorities and its clauses would be drawn up by them; that it be imposed upon the enemy and not discussed with him; that it be such as to prevent all resumption of hostilities and assure the submission of the vanquished to the terms of peace. So it was that the discussion went on with Berlin till October 23, and in Paris from that date till November 5. It was to the Commander-in-Chief [Foch] that final decision was left not only on the principle of the Armistice but upon its application. He it was who drew up the text. And it was his draft that was adopted. The action of the governments was limited to endorsing it and making it more severe. That is the truth:—it is perhaps less picturesque but certainly more in accord with common sense."

The terms of the Armistice were delivered to the Germans by Marshal Foch November 7, and they were given seventy-two hours to accept or reject them. Meanwhile Germany's allies were rapidly deserting her. Bulgaria surrendered September 30, and on October 30 Turkey signed an armistice. Finally on November 4, the rapidly disintegrating Austro-Hungarian Monarchy also signed an armistice. On October 28 there had been a naval mutiny at Kiel which spread rapidly to the other ports. On the 31st the Emperor departed for Army Headquarters, leaving Berlin on the verge of revolution. On the 7th of November the Social Democrats demanded the abdication of the Emperor and the Crown Prince. On the 9th Prince Max resigned the Chancellorship, and the Kaiser abdicated and ignominiously fled across the border into Holland. On the 11th at 5 A. M. the Armistice was signed by the German delegates and Marshal Foch, and it went into effect at 11 o'clock that day.

In two particulars the Wilson principles had been modified by the Allies. In the American note to Germany of November 5 Secretary Lansing stated that the President had submitted his correspondence with the German authorities to the Allied Governments and that he had received in reply the following memorandum:

"The Allied Governments have given careful consideration to the correspondence which has passed between the President of the United States and the German Government. Subject to the qualifications which follow, they declare their willingness to make peace with the Government of Germany on the terms of peace laid down in the President's Address to Congress of January 8, 1918, and the principles of settlement enunciated in his subsequent Addresses. They must point out, however, that Clause 2, relating to what is usually described as the freedom of the seas, is open to various interpretations, some of which they could not accept. They must therefore reserve to themselves complete freedom on this subject when they enter the Peace Conference. Further, in the conditions of peace laid down in his Address to Congress of January 8, 1918, the President declared that the invaded territories must be restored as well as evacuated and freed, and the Allied Governments feel that no doubt ought to be allowed to exist as to what this provision implies. By it they understand that compensation will be made by Germany for all damage done to the civilian population of the Allies and their property by the aggression of Germany by land, by sea, and from the air." In transmitting this memorandum Secretary Lansing stated that he was instructed by the President to say that he agreed with this interpretation.

With these modifications the Wilson principles were accepted by all parties as the legal basis of the peace negotiations.

XI

THE TREATY OF VERSAILLES

It was agreed that the Peace Conference should meet at Paris, and President Wilson considered the issues involved of such magnitude that he decided to head the American delegation himself. Great Britain, France, and Italy were to be represented by their premiers, and it was fitting that the United States should be represented by its most responsible leader, who, furthermore, had been the chief spokesman of the Allies and had formulated the principles upon which the peace was to be made. But the decision of the President to go to Paris was without precedent in our history and, therefore, it met with criticism and opposition. When he announced the names of the other members of the delegation, the criticism became even more outspoken and severe. They were Secretary of State Lansing, Henry White, former ambassador to France, Colonel Edward M. House, and General Tasker H. Bliss. There had been a widespread demand for a non-partisan peace commission, and many people thought that the President should have taken Root, or Roosevelt, or Taft. Mr. White was a Republican but he had never been active in party affairs or in any sense a leader. In the Senate there was deep resentment that the President had not selected any members of that body to accompany him. President McKinley had appointed three senators as members of the commission of five that negotiated the treaty of peace at the close of the Spanish War. With that exception, senators had never taken part directly in the negotiation of a treaty. The delegation was attended by a large group of experts on military, economic, geographical, ethnological, and legal matters, some of whom were men of great ability, and in their selection no party lines were drawn.

But just before the signing of the Armistice, the President had suffered a serious political defeat at home. There had been severe criticism of Democratic leadership in Congress and growing dissatisfaction with some of the members of the Cabinet. In response to the appeals of Democratic Congressmen, the President issued a statement from the White House on October 25, asking the people, if they approved of his leadership and wished him to continue to be their "unembarrassed spokesman in affairs at home and abroad," to vote for the Democratic candidates for Congress. He acknowledged that the Republicans in Congress had loyally supported his war measures, but he declared that they were hostile to the administration and that the time was too critical for divided leadership. This statement created a storm of criticism, and did more than any other act in his administration to turn the tide of public opinion against the President. The elections resulted in a Republican majority of thirty-nine in the House and two in the Senate. The President had followed the practice of European premiers in appealing to the people, but under our constitutional system he could not very well resign. Had he not issued his appeal, the election would have been regarded as a repudiation of the Democratic Congress, but not necessarily as a repudiation of the President. The situation was most unfortunate, but the President made no comments and soon after announced his intention of going to Paris. In December Lloyd George went to the country, and on pledging himself to make Germany pay for the war and to hang the Kaiser, he was returned by a substantial majority. These pledges were unnecessary and had a most unfortunate influence on the subsequent negotiations at Paris.

The President sailed for France December 4, leaving a divided country behind him. His enemies promptly seized the opportunity to assail him. Senator Sherman introduced a resolution declaring the presidency vacant because the President had left the territory of the United States, and Senator Knox offered another resolution declaring that the Conference should confine itself solely to the restoration of peace, and that the proposed league of nations should be reserved for consideration at some future time.

While his enemies in the Senate were busily organizing all the forces of opposition against him, the President was welcomed by the war-weary peoples of Europe with demonstrations of genuine enthusiasm such as had been the lot of few men in history to receive. Sovereigns and heads of States bestowed the highest honors upon him, while great crowds of working men gathered at the railroad stations in order to get a glimpse of the man who had led the crusade for a peace that would end war and establish justice as the rule of conduct between the nations of the world, great and small nations alike.

No mortal man could have fulfilled the hopes and expectations that centered in Wilson when he landed on the shores of France in December, 1918. The Armistice had been signed on the basis of his ideals, and the peoples of Europe confidently expected to see those ideals embodied in the treaty of peace. He still held the moral leadership of the world, but the war was over, the German menace ended, and national rivalries and jealousies were beginning to reappear, even among those nations who had so recently fought and bled side by side. This change was to be revealed when the Conference met. There was no sign of it in the plaudits of the multitudes who welcomed the President in France, in England, and in Italy. He returned on January 7, 1919, from Italy to Paris, where delegates to the Conference from all the countries which had been at war with Germany were gathering.

The first session of the Peace Conference was held January 18. The main work of the Conference was carried on by the Supreme Council, constituted at this meeting and composed of the two ranking delegates of each of the five great powers, Great Britain, France, Italy, the United States, and Japan. The decisions which this Council arrived at, with the aid of the large groups of technical advisers which accompanied the delegations of the great powers, were reported to the Conference in plenary session from time to time and ratified. The Supreme Council was, however, gradually superseded by the "Big Four," Wilson, Lloyd George, Clemenceau, and Orlando, while the "Five," composed of ministers of foreign affairs, handled much of the routine business, and made some important decisions, subject to the approval of the "Four." According to statistics compiled by Tardieu, the Council of Ten held seventy-two sessions, the "Five" held thirty-nine, and the "Four" held one hundred and forty-five. As one of the American experts puts it: "The 'Ten' fell into the background, the 'Five' never emerged from obscurity, the 'Four' ruled the Conference in the culminating period when its decisions took shape."

At the plenary session of January 25, President Wilson made a notable speech in which he proposed the creation of a league of nations, and a resolution to organize such a league and make it an integral part of the general treaty was unanimously adopted. A commission to draft a constitution for the League was appointed with President Wilson as chairman. On February 14 the first draft of the Covenant of the League was presented by him to the Conference, and on the following day he sailed for the United States in order to consider the bills passed by Congress before the expiration of the session on March 4. The first draft of the Covenant was hastily prepared, and it went back to the commission for revision. As soon as the text was made known in the United States, opposition to the Covenant was expressed in the Senate. During the President's brief visit to Washington, he gave a dinner at the White House to members of the Senate

Committee on Foreign Relations and of the House Committee on Foreign Affairs for the purpose of explaining to them the terms of the Covenant. There was no official report of what occurred at this dinner, but it was stated that some of the senators objected to the Covenant on the ground that it was contrary to our traditional policies and inconsistent with our Constitution and form of government. On March 4, the day before the President left New York to resume his duties at the Conference, Senators Lodge and Knox issued a round robin, signed by thirty-seven senators, declaring that they would not vote for the Covenant in the form proposed, and that consideration of the League of Nations should be postponed until peace had been concluded with Germany. That same night the President made a speech at the Metropolitan Opera House in New York City in which, after explaining and defining the Covenant, he said: "When that treaty comes back gentlemen on this side will find the Covenant not only in it, but so many threads of the treaty tied to the Covenant that you cannot dissect the Covenant from the treaty without destroying the whole vital structure." In this same address he also said: "The first thing I am going to tell the people on the other side of the water is that an overwhelming majority of the American people is in favour of the League of Nations. I know that this is true. I have had unmistakable intimations of it from all parts of the country, and the voice rings true in every case." The President was evidently quite confident that public sentiment would compel the Senate to ratify the peace treaty, including the Covenant of the League. A nation-wide propaganda was being carried on by the League to Enforce Peace and other organizations, and public sentiment for the League appeared to be overwhelming. The President took back to Paris with him various suggestions of changes in the Covenant, and later ex-President Taft, Elihu Root, and Charles E. Hughes proposed amendments which were forwarded to him and carefully considered by the commission. Some of these suggestions, such as the reservation of the Monroe Doctrine and the right of withdrawal from the League, were embodied in the final draft.

When the President returned to Paris he found that Secretary Lansing and Colonel House had consented to the separation of the League from the treaty of peace. He immediately reversed this decision, but the final adoption of the Covenant was delayed by the demand of Japan that a clause be inserted establishing "the principle of equality of nations and just treatment of their nationals," which would have brought within the jurisdiction of the League the status of Japan's subjects in California and in the British dominions. France urged the inclusion of a provision creating a permanent General Staff to direct the military operations of the League, and Belgium insisted that Brussels rather than Geneva should be the seat of the League. Meanwhile other national aspirations were also brought forward which delayed the general treaty of peace. France wanted the entire left bank of the Rhine; Italy put forth a claim to Fiume; and Japan, relying on secret agreements with England, France, and Italy, insisted on her claims to Shantung. No economic settlement had as yet been agreed upon, and the question of reparations was threatening the disruption of the Conference.

The most difficult problem that the Conference had to solve was the establishment of a new Franco-German frontier. There was no question about Alsace-Lorraine. That had been disposed of by the Fourteen Points, and Germany had acquiesced in its return to France in the pre-Armistice agreement. But no sooner was the Armistice signed than Foch addressed a note to Clemenceau, setting forth the necessity of making the Rhine the western frontier of Germany. The Left Bank, extending from Alsace-Lorraine to the Dutch frontier, embraced about 10,000 square miles and 5,500,000 people. The debate on this question continued at intervals for six months and at times became very acrimonious. The French representatives did not demand the direct annexation of the Left Bank, but they proposed an independent or autonomous Rhineland and French, or inter-Allied, occupation of the Rhine for an indefinite period, or at least until the full execution by Germany of the financial clauses of the treaty. Both the British and American delegates opposed the French proposals. Lloyd George repeatedly said: "We must not create another Alsace-Lorraine." He also remarked on one occasion: "The strongest impression made upon me by my first visit to Paris was the statue of Strasburg veiled in mourning. Do not let us make it possible for Germany to erect a similar statue."

This discussion was being carried on with great earnestness and intensity of feeling when Wilson returned to Paris March 14. That very afternoon he met Lloyd George and Clemenceau. The French argument was set forth again at length and with great skill. The fact was again pointed out that the destruction of the German fleet had relieved England from all fear of German invasion, and that the Atlantic Ocean lay between Germany and the United States, while France, which had suffered two German invasions in half a century, had no safeguard but the League of Nations, which she did not deem as good a guarantee as the Rhine bridges. Finally Wilson and Lloyd George offered the guarantee treaties, and Clemenceau agreed to take the proposal under consideration. Three days later he came back with a counter proposition and a compromise was reached. France gave up her demand for a separate Rhineland, but secured occupation of the Left Bank, including the bridge-heads, for a period of fifteen years as a guarantee of the execution of the treaty. In return the United States and Great Britain pledged themselves to come to the immediate aid of France, in case of an unprovoked attack, by an agreement which was to be binding only if ratified by both countries. This treaty the United States Senate refused to ratify. Foch was opposed to this compromise, and adopted a course of action which was very embarrassing to Clemenceau. Fierce attacks on the French Government and on the representatives of Great Britain and the United States, inspired by him, appeared in the papers. When the treaty was finally completed, he even went so far as to refuse to transmit the note summoning the German delegates to Versailles to receive it. Wilson and Lloyd George finally protested so vigorously to Clemenceau that Foch had to give way.

In view of the promises of Clemenceau and Lloyd George that Germany should pay the cost of the war, the question of reparations was an exceedingly difficult one to adjust. President Wilson stoutly opposed the inclusion of war costs as contrary to the pre-Armistice agreement, and Lloyd George and Clemenceau finally had to give in. The entire American delegation and their corps of experts endeavored to limit the charges imposed on Germany rigidly to reparation for damage done to civilians in the occupied areas and on land and sea. Lloyd George, remembering the promises which he had made prior to the December elections, insisted that pensions paid by the Allied governments should be included as damage done to the civilian population. This claim was utterly illogical, for pensions fall properly into the category of military expenses, but it was pressed with such skill and determination by Lloyd George and General Smuts that President Wilson finally gave his assent.

From the first the American delegates and experts were in favor of fixing definitely the amount that Germany was to pay in the way of reparations and settling this question once for all. They hoped to agree upon a sum which it was within Germany's power to pay. But Clemenceau and Lloyd George had made such extravagant promises to their people that they were afraid to announce at this time a sum which would necessarily be much less than the people expected. They, therefore, insisted that the question should be left open to be determined later by a Reparations Commission. They declared that any other course would mean the immediate overthrow of their governments and the reorganization of the British and French delegations. President Wilson did not care to put himself in the position of appearing to precipitate a political crisis in either country, so he finally gave way on this point also. These concessions proved to be the most serious mistakes that he made at Paris, for they did more than anything else to undermine the faith of liberals everywhere in him.

The Italian delegation advanced a claim to Fiume which was inconsistent both with the Treaty of London and the Fourteen Points. When disagreement over this question had been delaying for weeks the settlement of other matters, President Wilson finally made a public statement of his position which was virtually an appeal to the Italian people over the heads of their delegation. The entire delegation withdrew from the Conference and went home, but Premier Orlando received an almost unanimous vote of confidence from his parliament, and he was supported by an overwhelming tide of public sentiment throughout Italy. This was the first indication of Wilson's loss of prestige with the peoples of Europe.

As already stated, the Japanese had insisted on the insertion in the Covenant of the League of the principle of racial equality. It is very doubtful whether they ever expected to succeed in this. The probability is that they advanced this principle in order to compel concessions on other points. Japan's main demand was that the German leases and concessions in the Chinese province of Shantung should be definitely confirmed to her by the treaty. Two weeks after the outbreak of the World War, Japan had addressed an ultimatum to Germany to the effect that she immediately withdraw all German vessels from Chinese and Japanese waters and deliver not later than September 15 "to the Imperial Japanese authorities without condition or compensation the entire leased territory of Kiao-chau with a view to the eventual restoration of the same to China." In a statement issued to the press Count Okuma said:

"As Premier of Japan, I have stated and I now again state to the people of America and all the world that Japan has no ulterior motive or desire to secure more territory, no thought of depriving China or any other peoples of anything which they now possess."

The Germans had spent about $100,000,000 in improving Tsing-tau, the principal city of Kiao-chau, and they had no intention of surrendering. After a siege of two months the city was captured by the Japanese army and navy, assisted by a small force of British troops. This was the first act in the drama. On January 8, 1915, Japan suddenly presented to the Chinese government the now famous Twenty-one Demands, deliberately misrepresenting to the United States and other powers the nature of these demands. Among other things, Japan demanded not only that China should assent to any agreement in regard to Shantung that Japan and Germany might reach at the conclusion of the war, but that she should also grant to her greater rights and concessions in Shantung than Germany had enjoyed. China was finally forced to agree to these demands.

Japan's next step was to acquire from the Allies the assurance that they would support her claims to Shantung and to the islands in the Pacific north of the equator on the conclusion of the war. This she did in secret agreements signed in February and March, 1917, with England, France, Italy, and Russia. England agreed to support Japan's claim on condition that Japan would support her claims to the Pacific islands south of the equator. France signed on condition that Japan would use her influence on China to break relations with Germany and place at the disposal of the Allies the German ships interned in Chinese ports. The Allies were evidently uneasy about Japan, and were willing to do anything that was necessary to satisfy her. This uncertainty about Japan may also be the explanation of the Lansing-Ishii agreement signed November 2, 1917, in which the United States recognized the "special interests" of Japan in China.

The secret treaties of the Allies relating to the Japanese claims were not revealed until the disposition of the German islands in the Pacific was under discussion at the Peace Conference. When informed by Baron Makino that the islands north of the equator had been pledged to Japan by agreements signed two years before, President Wilson inquired whether there were other secret agreements, and was informed that the German rights in Shantung had also been promised to Japan. As the other powers were pledged to support Japan's claims, President Wilson found himself in a very embarrassing situation, especially as he had also to oppose Japan's demand that a clause recognizing racial equality be inserted in the Covenant of the League. This was a moral claim that Japan urged with great strategic effect. In pushing her claims to Shantung she ignored all moral considerations and relied entirely upon her legal status, secured (1) by the secret treaties with the Allies, (2) by the treaty of 1915 with China, and (3) by right of conquest. When charged with having coerced China into signing the treaty of 1915, Japan replied with truth that most of the important treaties with China had been extorted by force. Japan declared, however, that she had no intention of holding Shantung permanently, but that she would restore the province in full sovereignty to China, retaining only the economic privileges transferred from Germany. In view of this oral promise, President Wilson finally acquiesced in the recognition of Japan's legal status in Shantung.

On May 7 the completed treaty was presented to the German delegates who had been summoned to Versailles to receive it. When the text was made public in Berlin there was an indignant outcry against the alleged injustice of certain provisions which were held to be inconsistent with the pledges given by President Wilson in the pre-Armistice negotiations, and the Germans made repeated efforts to draw the Allies into a general discussion of principles. They were, however, finally given to understand that they must accept or reject the treaty as it stood, and on June 28 it was signed in the Hall of Mirrors at Versailles—the same hall in which William I had been crowned Emperor of Germany forty-eight years before.

The next day President Wilson sailed for the United States, and on July 10 personally presented the treaty to the Senate with an earnest appeal for prompt ratification. The Committee on Foreign Relations, to which the treaty was referred, proceeded with great deliberation, and on July 31 began a series of public hearings which lasted until September 12. The Committee called before it Secretary Lansing and several of the technical advisors to the American delegation, including B. M. Baruch, economic adviser, Norman H. Davis, financial adviser, and David Hunter Miller, legal adviser. The Committee also called before it a number of American citizens who had had no official connection with the negotiations but who wished to speak in behalf of foreign groups, including Thomas F. Millard for China, Joseph W. Folk for Egypt, Dudley Field Malone for India, and a large delegation of Americans of Irish descent, who opposed the League of Nations on the ground that it would stand in the way of Ireland's aspiration for independence. The rival claims of Jugo-Slavs and Italians to Fiume, the demand of Albania for self-determination, the claims of Greece to Thrace, and arguments for and against the separation of Austria and Hungary were all presented at great length to the Committee. On August 19 the President received the Committee at the White House, and after submitting a written statement on certain features of the Covenant, he was questioned by members of the Committee and a general discussion followed.

Meanwhile, the treaty was being openly debated in the Senate. The President had been an advocate of publicity in diplomacy as well as in other things, and the Senate now undertook to use his own weapon against him by a public attack on the treaty. Although the opposition to the treaty was started in the Senate by Lodge, Borah, Johnson, Sherman, Reed, and Poindexter, it was not confined to that body. Throughout the country there were persons of liberal views who favored the League of Nations but objected to the severe terms imposed on Germany, and charged the President with having proved false to the principles of the Fourteen Points. There were others who did not object to a severe peace, but who were bound fast by the tradition of isolation and thought membership in the League of Nations would involve the sacrifice of national sovereignty. The main object of attack was Article X, which guaranteed the territorial integrity and political independence of all the members of the League. President Wilson stated to the Senate Committee that he regarded Article X as "the very backbone of the whole Covenant," and that "without it the League would be hardly more than an influential debating society." The opponents of the League declared that this article would embroil the United States in the internal affairs of Europe, and that it deprived Congress of its constitutional right to declare war.

In the Senate there were three groups: the small number of "irreconcilables" who opposed the ratification of the treaty in any form; a larger group who favored ratification without amendments, but who finally expressed their willingness to accept "interpretative reservations"; and a large group composed mainly of Republicans who favored the ratification of the treaty only on condition that there should be attached to it reservations safeguarding what they declared to be the fundamental rights and interests of the United States. This group differed among themselves as to the character of the reservations that were necessary, and some of them became known as "mild reservationists."

It is probable that at the outset only the small group of "irreconcilables" hoped or intended to bring about the defeat of the treaty, but as the debate proceeded and the opposition to the treaty received more and more popular support, the reservationists determined to defeat the treaty altogether rather than to accept any compromise. The Republican leaders were quick to realize that the tide of public opinion had turned and was now running strongly against the President. They determined, therefore, to ruin him at all hazards, and thus to bring about the election of a Republican president.

When President Wilson realized that the treaty was really in danger of defeat, he determined to go on an extended tour of the country for the purpose of explaining the treaty to the people and bringing pressure to bear on the Senate. Beginning at Columbus, Ohio, on September 4, he proceeded through the northern tier of states to the Pacific coast, then visited California and returned through Colorado. He addressed large audiences who received him with great enthusiasm. He was "trailed" by Senator Hiram Johnson, who was sent out by the opposition in the Senate to present the other side. Johnson also attracted large crowds. On the return trip, while delivering an address at Wichita, Kansas, September 26, the President showed signs of a nervous breakdown and returned immediately to Washington. He was able to walk from the train to his automobile, but a few days later he was partially paralyzed. The full extent and seriousness of his illness was carefully concealed from the public. He was confined to the White House for five months, and had to abandon all efforts in behalf of the treaty.

On September 10 the Committee on Foreign Relations reported the treaty to the Senate with a number of amendments and reservations. The Committee declared that the League was an alliance, and that it would "breed wars instead of securing peace." They also declared that the Covenant demanded "sacrifices of American independence and sovereignty which would in no way promote the world's peace," and that the amendments and reservations which they proposed were intended "to guard American rights and American sovereignty." The following day the minority members of the Committee submitted a report opposing both amendments and reservations. A few days later Senator McCumber presented a third report representing the views of the "mild reservationists." It objected to the phraseology of the Committee's reservations as unnecessarily severe and recommended substitute reservations. The treaty then became the regular order in the Senate and was read section by section and debated each day for over two months. The amendments of the text of the treaty were all rejected by substantial majorities for the reason that their adoption would have made it necessary to resubmit the treaty not only to the Allies but also to Germany. The majority of the senators were opposed to such a course. The Committee, therefore, decided to substitute reservations for amendments, and Senator Lodge finally submitted, on behalf of the Committee, fourteen reservations preceded by a preamble, which declared that the ratification of the treaty was not to take effect or bind the United States until these reservations had been accepted as a condition of ratification by at least three of the four principal Allied and associated powers, namely, Great Britain, France, Italy, and Japan.

The first reservation provided that in case of withdrawal from the League the United States should be the sole judge as to whether its international obligations under the Covenant had been fulfilled. This reservation was adopted by a vote of 50 to 35.

The second reservation declared that the United States assumed no obligation to preserve the territorial integrity or political independence of any other country or to interfere in controversies between nations under the provisions of Article X "or to employ the military or naval forces of the United States under any article of the treaty for any purpose, unless in any particular case the Congress, which, under the Constitution, has the sole power to declare war or authorize the employment of the military or naval forces of the United States, shall by act or joint resolution so provide." This reservation was adopted by a vote of 46 to 33.

Reservation Number 3, providing that no mandate under the treaty should be accepted by the United States except by action of Congress, was adopted by a vote of 52 to 31.

Number 4, excluding domestic questions from consideration by the Council or the Assembly of the League, was adopted by a vote of 59 to 26.

Number 5, declaring the Monroe Doctrine "to be wholly outside the jurisdiction of said League of Nations and entirely unaffected by any provision contained in said treaty of peace with Germany," and reserving to the United States the sole right to interpret the Monroe Doctrine, was adopted by a vote of 55 to 34.

Number 6, withholding the assent of the United States from the provisions of the treaty relating to Shantung and reserving full liberty of action with respect to any controversy which might arise under said articles between China and Japan, was adopted by a vote of 53 to 41.

Number 7, reserving to Congress the right to provide by law for the appointment of the representatives of the United States in the Assembly and Council of the League and members of commissions, committees or courts under the League, and requiring the confirmation of all by the Senate, was adopted by a vote of 53 to 40.

Number 8, declaring that the Reparations Commission should not be understood as having the right to regulate or interfere with exports from the United States to Germany or from Germany to the United States without an act or joint resolution of Congress, was adopted by a vote of 54 to 40.

Number 9, declaring that the United States should not be under any obligation to contribute to any of the expenses of the League without an act of Congress, was adopted by a vote of 56 to 39.

Number 10, providing that if the United States should at any time adopt any plan for the limitation of armaments proposed by the Council of the League, it reserved "the right to increase such armaments without the consent of the Council whenever the United States is threatened with invasion or engaged in war," was adopted by a vote of 56 to 39.

Number 11, reserving the right of the United States to permit the nationals of a Covenant-breaking State residing within the United States to continue their commercial, financial, and personal relations with the nationals of the United States, was adopted by a vote of 53 to 41.

Number 12, relating to the very complicated question of private debts, property rights and interests of American citizens, was adopted by a vote of 52 to 41.

Number 13, withholding the assent of the United States from the entire section of the treaty relating to international labor organization until Congress should decide to participate, was adopted by a vote of 54 to 35.

Number 14 declared that the United States would not be bound by any action of the Council or Assembly in which any member of the League and its self-governing dominions or colonies should cast in the aggregate more than one vote. This reservation was adopted by a vote of 55 to 38.

A number of other reservations were offered and rejected. Under the rules of the Senate, amendments and reservations to a treaty may be adopted by a majority vote, while a treaty can be ratified only by a two-thirds vote. A number of senators who were opposed to the treaty voted for the Lodge reservations in order to insure its defeat. When the vote on the treaty with the reservations was taken November 19, it stood 39 for and 55 against. A motion to reconsider the vote was then adopted, and Senator Hitchcock, the Democratic leader, proposed five reservations covering the right of withdrawal, domestic questions, the Monroe Doctrine, the right of Congress to decide on the employment of the naval and military forces of the United States in any case arising under Article X, and restrictions on the voting powers of self-governing colonies or dominions. These reservations were rejected, the vote being 41 to 50. Another vote was then taken on the treaty with the Lodge reservations, the result being 41 for and 51 against. Senator Underwood then offered a resolution to ratify the treaty without reservations of any kind. The vote on this resolution was 38 for and 53 against.

It was now evident that there was little prospect of securing the ratification of the treaty without compromise. On January 8, 1920, a letter from the President was read at the Jackson Day dinner in Washington, in which he refused to accept the decision of the Senate as final and said: "There can be no reasonable objection to interpretations accompanying the act of ratification itself. But when the treaty is acted upon, I must know whether it means that we have ratified or rejected it. We cannot rewrite this treaty. We must take it without changes which alter its meaning, or leave it, and then, after the rest of the world has signed it, we must face the unthinkable task of making another and separate kind of treaty with Germany." In conclusion he declared: "If there is any doubt as to what the people of the country think on this vital matter, the clear and single way out is to submit it for determination at the next election to the voters of the nation, to give the next election the form of a great and solemn referendum, a referendum as to the part the United States is to play in completing the settlements of the war and in the prevention in the future of such outrages as Germany attempted to perpetrate."

During the last week of January a compromise was discussed by an informal by-partisan committee, and the President wrote a letter saying he would accept the Hitchcock reservations, but Lodge refused to accept any compromise. On February 9 the Senate again referred the treaty to the Committee on Foreign Relations with instructions to report it back immediately with the reservations previously adopted. After several weeks of fruitless debate a fifteenth reservation, expressing sympathy for Ireland, was added to the others, by a vote of 38 to 36. It was as follows: "In consenting to the ratification of the treaty with Germany the United States adheres to the principle of self-determination and to the resolution of sympathy with the aspirations of the Irish people for a government of their own choice adopted by the Senate June 6, 1919, and declares that when such government is obtained by Ireland, a consummation it is hoped is at hand, it should promptly be admitted as a member of the League of Nations."

With a few changes in the resolutions previously adopted and an important change in the preamble, the ratifying resolution was finally put to the vote March 19, 1920. The result was 49 votes for and 35 against. On the following day the secretary of the Senate was instructed by a formal resolution to return the treaty to the President and to inform him that the Senate had failed to ratify it.

The treaty thus became the leading issue in the presidential campaign, but unfortunately it was not the only issue. The election proved to be a referendum on the Wilson administration as a whole rather than on the treaty. The Republican candidate, Senator Harding, attacked the Wilson administration for its arbitrary and unconstitutional methods and advocated a return to "normalcy." He denounced the Wilson League as an attempt to set up a super-government, but said he favored an association of nations and an international court. Governor Cox, the Democratic candidate, came out strongly for the treaty, particularly during the latter part of his campaign. The result was an overwhelming victory for Harding. President Wilson had been too ill to take any part in the campaign. His administration had been the chief issue, and the people had, certainly for the time being, repudiated it. He accepted the result philosophically and refrained from comments, content, apparently, to leave the part he had played in world affairs to the verdict of history. In December, 1920, the Nobel Peace Prize was awarded to him as a foreign recognition of the services he had rendered to humanity.

XII

THE WASHINGTON CONFERENCE

After the rejection of the Treaty of Versailles by the Senate, President Wilson withdrew as far as possible from participation in European affairs, and after the election of Harding he let it be known that he would do nothing to embarrass the incoming administration. The public had been led to believe that when Harding became President there would be a complete reversal of our foreign policy all along the line, but such was not to be the case. The new administration continued unchanged the Wilson policy toward Mexico and toward Russia, and before many months had passed was seeking from Congress the authority, withheld from Wilson, to appoint a member on the Reparations Commission. On the question of our rights in mandated areas, Secretary Hughes adopted in whole the arguments which had been advanced by Secretary Colby in his note to Great Britain of November 20, 1920, in regard to the oil resources of Mesopotamia. By the San Remo agreement of April 25, 1920, Great Britain and France had agreed upon a division of the oil output of Mesopotamia by which France was to be allowed 25 per cent. and Great Britain 75 per cent. The British Government had intimated that the United States, having declined to join the League of Nations, had no voice in the matter. On this point Secretary Colby took sharp issue in the following statement: "Such powers as the Allied and Associated nations may enjoy or wield, in the determination of the governmental status of the mandated areas, accrued to them as a direct result of the war against the Central Powers. The United States, as a participant in that conflict and as a contributor to its successful issue, cannot consider any of the Associated Powers, the smallest not less than herself, debarred from the discussion of any of its consequences, or from participation in the rights and privileges secured under the mandates provided for in the treaties of peace."

Japan likewise assumed that we had nothing to do with the disposition of the former German islands in the Pacific. When the Supreme Council at Paris decided to give Japan a mandate over the islands north of the equator, President Wilson reserved for future consideration the final disposition of the island of Yap, which lies between Guam and the Philippines, and is one of the most important cable stations in the Pacific. The entire question of cable communications was reserved for a special conference which met at Washington in the autumn of 1920, but this conference adjourned about the middle of December without having reached any final conclusions, and the status of Yap became the subject of a very sharp correspondence between the American and Japanese governments. When Hughes became Secretary of State, he restated the American position in a note of April 2, 1921, as follows:

"It will not be questioned that the right to dispose of the overseas possessions of Germany was acquired only through the victory of the Allied and Associated Powers, and it is also believed that there is no disposition on the part of the Japanese Government to deny the participation of the United States in that victory. It would seem to follow necessarily that the right accruing to the Allied and Associated Powers through the common victory is shared by the United States and that there could be no valid or effective disposition of the overseas possessions of Germany, now under consideration, without the assent of the United States."

The discussion between the two governments was still in progress when the Washington Conference convened, and at the close of the Conference it was announced that an agreement had been reached which would be embodied in a treaty. The United States recognized Japan's mandate over the islands north of the equator on the condition that the United States should have full cable rights on the island of Yap, and that its citizens should enjoy certain rights of residence on the island. The agreement also covered radio telegraphic service.

During the presidential campaign Harding's position on the League of Nations had been so equivocal that the public knew not what to expect, but when Hughes and Hoover were appointed members of the Cabinet, it was generally expected that the new administration would go into the League with reservations. This expectation was not to be fulfilled, however, for the President persistently ignored the existence of the League, and took no notice of the establishment of the permanent Court of International Justice provided for in Article 14 of the Covenant. Meanwhile Elihu Root, who as Secretary of State had instructed our delegates to the Hague Conference of 1907 to propose the establishment of such a court, had been invited by the Council of the League to be one of a commission of distinguished jurists to draft the statute establishing the court. This service he performed with conspicuous ability. As another evidence of Europe's unwillingness to leave us out, when the court was organized John Bassett Moore, America's most distinguished authority on international law, was elected one of the judges.

Meanwhile a technical state of war with Germany existed and American troops were still on the Rhine. On July 2, 1921, Congress passed a joint resolution declaring the war at an end, but undertaking to reserve to the United States "all rights, privileges, indemnities, reparations or advantages" to which it was entitled under the terms of the Armistice, or by reason of its participation in the war, or which had been stipulated for its benefit in the

Treaty of Versailles, or to which it was entitled as one of the Principal Allied and Associated Powers, or to which it was entitled by virtue of any act or acts of Congress. On August 25 the United States Government, through its commissioner to Germany, signed at Berlin a separate treaty of peace with Germany, reserving in detail the rights referred to in the joint resolution of Congress. About the same time a similar treaty was signed with Austria, and the two treaties were ratified by the Senate of the United States October 18. The proclamation of peace produced no immediate results of any importance. American troops continued on the Rhine, and there was no apparent increase in trade, which had been carried on before the signing of the treaty by special licenses.

If mankind is capable of learning any lessons from history, the events leading up to the World War should have exploded the fallacy that the way to preserve peace is to prepare for war. Competition in armament, whether on land or sea, inevitably leads to war, and it can lead to nothing else. And yet, after the terrible lessons of the recent war, the race for armaments continued with increased momentum. France, Russia, and Poland maintained huge armies, while the United States and Japan entered upon the most extensive naval construction programs in the history of the world. Great Britain, burdened with debt, was making every effort to keep pace with the United States.

This naval rivalry between powers which had so lately been united in the war against Germany, led thoughtful people to consider the probable outcome and to ask against whom these powers were arming. We had no quarrel with England, but England was the ally of Japan, and relations between Japan and the United States in the Pacific and in Eastern Asia were far from reassuring. The question of the continuance of the Anglo-Japanese Alliance was discussed at the British Imperial Conference, which met at London in the early summer of 1921. The original purpose of this compact was to check the Russian advance in Manchuria. It was renewed in revised form in 1905 against Germany, and again renewed in 1911 against Germany for a period of ten years. With the removal of the German menace, what reasons were there for Great Britain to continue the alliance? It bore too much the aspect of a combination against the United States, and was of course the main reason for the naval program which we had adopted. So long as there were only three navies of importance in the world and two of them united in a defensive alliance, it behooved us to safeguard our position as a sea power.

One of the main objects of the formation of the League of Nations was to bring about a limitation of armaments on land and sea, and a commission was organized under the League to consider this question, but this commission could not take any steps toward the limitation of navies so long as a great naval power like the United States refused to coöperate with the League of Nations or even to recognize its existence. As President Harding had promised the American people some substitute for the League of Nations, he decided, soon after coming into office, to convene an international conference to consider the limitation of armament on land and sea. By the time the Conference convened it was evident that no agreement was possible on the subject of land armament. It was recognized from the first that the mere proposal to limit navies would be utterly futile unless effective steps could be taken to remove some of the causes of international conflict which make navies necessary. Therefore the formal invitation to the Conference extended to the governments of Great Britain, France, Italy and Japan, August 11, 1921, linked the subject of Limitation of Armament with Pacific and Far Eastern Questions. The European powers accepted the invitation without much enthusiasm, but Japan's answer was held back for some time. She was reluctant to have the powers review the course she had pursued in China and Siberia while they were at war with Germany. After agreeing to attend the Conference, Japan endeavored to confine the program to as narrow limits as possible, and she soon entered into negotiations with China over the Shantung question with the hope of arriving at a settlement which would prevent that question from coming before the Conference. Invitations to the Conference were later sent to the governments of Belgium, the Netherlands, Portugal, and China. Portugal was interested because of her settlement at Macao, the oldest European settlement in China. Holland of course is one of the great colonial powers of the Pacific. While Belgium has no territorial interests in the Orient, she has for years been interested in Chinese financial matters.

The Washington Conference convened in plenary session November 12, 1921, in Memorial Continental Hall. Seats were reserved on the main floor for press representatives, and the galleries were reserved for officials and those individuals who were fortunate enough to secure tickets of admission. The question of open diplomacy which had been much discussed, was settled at the first session by Secretary Hughes, who, in his introductory speech, boldly laid the American proposals for the limitation of navies before the Conference. There were in all seven plenary sessions, but the subsequent sessions did little more than confirm agreements that had already been reached in committee. The real work of the Conference was carried on by committees, and from the meetings of these committees the public and press representatives were as a matter of course excluded. There were two principal committees, one on the Limitation of Armament, and the other on Pacific and Far Eastern Questions. There were various sub-committees, in the work of which technical delegates participated. Minutes were kept of the meetings of the two principal committees, and after each meeting a communiqué was prepared for the press. In fact, the demand for publicity defeated to a large extent its own ends. So much matter was given to the press that when it was published in full very few people had time to read it. As a general rule, the less real information there was to give out, the longer were the communiqués. Experienced correspondents maintained that decisions on delicate questions were made with as much secrecy in Washington as at Paris.

The plan of the United States for the limitation of armament presented by Secretary Hughes at the first session proposed (1) that all programs for the construction of capital ships, either actual or projected, be abandoned; (2) that a large number of battleships of older types still in commission be scrapped; and (3) that the allowance of auxiliary combatant craft, such as cruisers, destroyers, submarines, and airplane carriers, be in proportion to the tonnage of capital ships. These proposals, it was claimed, would leave the powers under consideration in the same relative positions. Under this plan the United States would be allowed 500,000 tons of capital ships, Great Britain 500,000 tons, and Japan 300,000 tons.

Japan objected to the 5-5-3 ratio proposed by Secretary Hughes, and urged a 10-10-7 ratio as more in accord with existing strength. The American proposal included the scrapping of the *Mutsu*, the pride of the Japanese navy, which had been launched but not quite completed. The sacrifices voluntarily proposed by the United States for its navy were much greater than those which England or Japan were called upon to make, and in this lay the strength of the American position. The Japanese refused, however, to give up the *Mutsu*, and they were finally permitted to retain it, but in order to preserve the 5-5-3 ratio, it was necessary to increase the tonnage allowance of the United States and Great Britain. In the treaty as finally agreed upon, Japan was allowed 315,000 tons of capital ships and the United States and Great Britain each 525,000 tons.

In his address at the opening session, Secretary Hughes said: "In view of the extraordinary conditions due to the World War affecting the existing strength of the navies of France and Italy, it is not thought to be necessary to discuss at this stage of the proceedings the tonnage allowance of these nations, but the United States proposes that this subject be reserved for the later consideration of the Conference." This somewhat blunt, matter-of-fact way of stating the case gave unexpected offense to the French delegation. During the next four or five weeks, while Great Britain, the United States, and Japan were discussing the case of the *Mutsu* and the question of fortifications in the Pacific, the French delegates were cherishing their resentment at being treated as the representatives of a second-class power. Hughes's failure to regard the susceptibilities of a great nation like France undoubtedly had a good deal to do with the upsetting of that part of the naval program relating to subsidiary craft and submarines.

When, after the agreement on the 5-5-3 ratio, the question of the allowance of capital ship tonnage for France and Italy was taken up in committee, the other powers were wholly unprepared for France's demand of 350,000 tons of capital ships. According to Hughes's figures based on existing strength, she was entitled to 175,000 tons. It is not probable that the French delegates intended to insist on such a large tonnage. It is more likely that they put forth this proposal in the committee in order to give the other delegates to understand that France could not be ignored or dictated to with impunity and in order to pave the way for their submarine proposal. Unfortunately the French demands were given to the press through some misunderstanding and caused an outburst of criticism in the British and American papers. In the committee the relations between the British and French delegates became very bitter over the refusal of the latter to abandon the submarine, or even agree to a moderate proposal as to submarine tonnage. On December 16 Secretary Hughes cabled an appeal, over the heads of the French delegation, to Briand, who had returned to Paris. As a result, the French finally agreed to accept the 1.75 ratio for capital ships, but refused to place any reasonable limits upon cruisers, destroyers, submarines, or aircraft. Italy accepted the same ratio as France.

Thus an important part of the Hughes program failed. As a result, the treaty leaves the contracting parties free to direct their energies, if they so desire, to the comparatively new fields of submarine and aerial warfare. As is well known, many eminent naval authorities, such as Sir Percy Scott in England and Admiral Sims in this country, believe that the capital ship is an obsolete type, and that the warfare of the future will be carried on by submarines, aircraft, and lighter surface ships. The unfortunate feature of the situation created by the naval treaty is, therefore, that those who regard the capital ship as obsolete will now have an opportunity to bring forward and press their submarine and aircraft programs. There is no limitation upon the building of cruisers, provided they do not exceed 10,000 tons displacement or carry guns with a calibre exceeding eight inches.

By Article 19 of the naval treaty the United States, Great Britain, and Japan agreed to maintain the *status quo* as regards fortifications and naval bases in the islands of the Pacific with certain exceptions, notably the Hawaiian Islands, Australia, and New Zealand. This agreement relieves Japan of all fear of attack from us, and let us hope that it may prove as beneficent and as enduring as the agreement of 1817 between the United States and Great Britain for disarmament on the Great Lakes.

The 5-5-3 ratio puts the navies of Great Britain, the United States, and Japan, for the present at least, on a strictly defensive basis. Each navy is strong enough to defend its home territory, but no one of them will be able to attack the home territory of the others. Of course it is possible that the development of aircraft and submarines, together with cruisers and other surface craft, may eventually alter the situation. Hitherto navies have existed for two purposes: national defense and the enforcement of foreign policies. The new treaty means that as long as it lasts the navies of the ratifying powers can be used for defense only and not for the enforcement of their policies in distant quarters of the globe. In other words, when disputes arise, British policies will prevail in the British area, American policies in the American area, and Japanese policies in the Japanese area. Having agreed to place ourselves in a position in which we cannot attack Japan, the only pressure we can bring to bear upon her in China or elsewhere is moral pressure. Through what was considered by some a grave strategical error, the naval treaty was completed before any settlement of the Chinese and Siberian questions had been reached.

The French insistence on the practically unlimited right to build submarines caused much hard feeling in England. The British delegates had proposed the total abolition of submarines, and this proposal had been ably supported by the arguments of Mr. Balfour and Lord Lee. Unfortunately the United States delegation stood for the submarine, proposing merely certain limits upon its use. The five naval powers finally signed a treaty reaffirming the old rules of international law in regard to the search and seizure of merchant vessels, and declaring that "any person in the service of any Power who shall violate any of those rules, whether or not such person is under orders of a governmental superior, shall be deemed to have violated the laws of war and shall be liable to trial and punishment as if for an act of piracy and may be brought to trial before the civil or military authorities of any Power within the jurisdiction of which he may be found." By the same treaty the signatory powers solemnly bound themselves to prohibit the use in war of poisonous gases.

The attempt to limit by treaty the use of the submarine and to prohibit altogether the use of gases appears to many to be utterly futile. After the experience of the late war, no nation would readily trust the good faith of another in these matters. Each party to a war would probably feel justified in being prepared to use the submarine and poison gases, contrary to law, in case the other party should do so. We would thus have the same old dispute as in the late war in regard to floating mines as to which party first resorted to the outlawed practice. What is the use in solemnly declaring that a submarine shall not attack a merchant vessel, and that the commander of a submarine who violates this law shall be treated as a pirate, when the contracting parties found it utterly impossible to agree among themselves upon a definition of a merchant vessel?

But the reader may ask, what is the use in signing any treaty if nations are so devoid of good faith? The answer is that the vast majority of treaties are faithfully kept in time of peace, but that very few treaties are fully observed in time of war. Had these five powers signed a treaty pledging themselves not to build or maintain submarines of any kind or description, we would have every reason to expect them to live up to it. But when a nation is engaged in war and has a large flotilla of submarines which it has agreed to use only for certain purposes, there is apt to come a time when the temptation to use them for wholly different purposes will be overwhelming.

The Committee on Pacific and Far Eastern Questions held its first meeting November 16. This committee was primarily concerned with the very delicate situation created by the aggressive action and expansion of Japan during the past twenty years. In 1905, by the Treaty of Portsmouth, Japan succeeded to the Russian rights in southern Manchuria; in 1910 she annexed Korea; in 1911, during the Chinese Revolution, she stationed troops at Hankow and later constructed permanent barracks; in 1914, after the defeat of the Germans at Kiao-chau, she took over all the German interests in the Shantung peninsula; in 1915 she presented the Twenty-one Demands to China and coerced that power into granting most of them; and in 1918, in conjunction with the United States, Great Britain, and France, she landed a military force in the Maritime Province of Siberia for the definite purpose of rescuing the Czecho-Slovak troops who had made their way to that province and of guarding the military stores at Vladivostok. The other powers had all withdrawn their contingents, but Japan had increased her force from one division to more than 70,000 troops. The eastern coast of Asia was thus in the firm grip of Japan, and she had secured concessions from China which seriously impaired the independence of that country.

It was commonly supposed that the United States delegation had prepared a program on the Far Eastern question, and that this would be presented in the same way that Hughes had presented the naval program. If this was the intention there was a sudden change of plan, for between one and two o'clock at night the Chinese delegates were aroused from their slumbers and informed that there would be an opportunity for them to present China's case before the committee at eleven o'clock that morning. They at once went to work with their advisers, and a few minutes before the appointed hour they completed the drafting of the Ten Points, which Minister Sze read before the committee. These Points constituted a Chinese declaration of independence, and set forth a series of general principles to be applied in the determination of questions relating to China. Several days later the committee adopted four resolutions, presented by Mr. Root, covering in part some of the Chinese principles. By these resolutions the powers agreed to respect the independence and territorial integrity of China, to give China the fullest opportunity to develop and maintain an effective and stable government, to recognize the principle of equality for the commerce and industry of all nations throughout the territory of China, and to refrain from taking advantage of present conditions in order to seek special rights or privileges. This somewhat vague and general declaration of principles appeared to be all that China was likely to get. Had Mr. Hughes presented a Far Eastern program and gotten nothing more than this, it would have been a serious blow to the prestige of the United States. That is probably why he decided at the last moment to let China present her own case.

At the fourth plenary session of the Conference the treaty relating to the Pacific islands, generally known as the Four-Power Treaty, was presented by Senator Lodge. By the terms of this treaty, the United States, Great Britain, France, and Japan agreed "to respect their rights in relation to their insular possessions and insular dominions in the region of the Pacific Ocean," and in case of any dispute arising out of any Pacific question to refer the matter to a joint conference for consideration and adjustment. This article appeared harmless enough, but Article 2 seemed to lay the foundations of an alliance between these powers. It was as follows: "If the said rights are threatened by the aggressive action of any other Power, the High Contracting Parties shall communicate with one another fully and frankly in order to arrive at an understanding as to the most efficient measures to be taken, jointly or separately, to meet the exigencies of the particular situation." This treaty is to remain in force for ten years, after which it may be terminated by any of the High Contracting Parties on twelve months' notice. It supersedes the Anglo-Japanese Alliance which, it expressly provided, should terminate on the exchange of ratifications.

In presenting the treaty, Senator Lodge assured his hearers that "no military or naval sanction lurks anywhere in the background or under cover of these plain and direct clauses," and Secretary Hughes in closing the discussion declared that it would probably not be possible to find in all history "an international document couched in more simple or even briefer terms," but he added, "we are again reminded that the great things are the simple ones." In view of these statements the members of the Conference and the public generally were completely flabbergasted some days later when Secretary Hughes and the President gave out contradictory statements as to whether the treaty included the Japanese homeland. Hughes stated to the correspondents that it did, the President said it did not. Whereupon

Since the middle of the last century Chinese tariffs have been regulated by treaties with foreign powers, the customs service organized and administered by foreigners, and the receipts mortgaged to meet the interest on foreign loans. China has never been permitted to levy duties in excess of 5 per cent., and, in fact, as a result of the methods of valuation the duties have not averaged above 3 1/2 per cent. This has been an unjust state of affairs, and has deprived the Chinese Government of what would naturally be one of its main sources of revenue. By the new agreement there is to be an immediate revision of tariff valuations so as to make the 5 per cent. effective. China is also to be allowed to levy a surtax on certain articles, mainly luxuries, which will yield an additional revenue. It is estimated that the total annual increase in revenue derived from maritime customs will be about $150,000,000 silver. It is claimed by some, with a certain degree of truth, that any increase in Chinese customs duties will be immediately covered by liens to secure new loans, and that putting money into the Chinese treasury just now is like pouring it into a rat hole. As soon as China is able to establish a stable and honest government, she should, without question, be relieved of all treaty restrictions on her tariffs.

The Conference also took certain steps to restore to China other sovereign rights long impaired by the encroachments of foreign powers. A commission is to be appointed to investigate the administration of justice with a view to the ultimate extinction of extraterritorial rights now enjoyed by foreigners. The powers also agreed to abandon not later than January 1, 1923, their existing postal agencies in China, provided an efficient Chinese postal service be maintained. The system of foreign post offices in China has been the subject of great abuses, as through these agencies goods of various kinds, including opium and other drugs, have been smuggled into China. The powers further made a general promise to aid the Chinese Government in the unification of railways into a general system under

Chinese control. They also agreed to restore to China all radio stations other than those regulated by treaty or maintained by foreign governments within their legation limits.

In the treaty relating to the open door, the Contracting Powers other than China pledged themselves to the following principles:

"(1) To respect the sovereignty, the independence, and the territorial and administrative integrity of China;

"(2) To provide the fullest and most unembarrassed opportunity to China to develop and maintain for herself an effective and stable government;

"(3) To use their influence for the purpose of effectually establishing and maintaining the principle of equal opportunity for the commerce and industry of all nations throughout the territory of China;

"(4) To refrain from taking advantage of conditions in China in order to seek special rights or privileges which would abridge the rights of subjects or citizens of friendly States, and from countenancing action inimical to the security of such States."

China on her part accepted fully the principle of the open door, and pledged herself for the first time to respect it. Pledges to respect the open door in China have been made by foreign powers upon various occasions in the past and broken as often as made. The expression "equal opportunity for the commerce and industry of all nations" is not new. It occurs in the Anglo-Japanese Alliance of 1902, in the Root-Takahira agreement of 1908, and in numerous other documents. In recent years, however, the United States has been the only power which has tried to preserve the open door in China. Most of the other powers have regarded the Chinese situation as hopeless, and have believed that the only solution was to let foreign powers come in and divide and rule the territory of the empire. In view of the new treaty the open door is no longer merely an American policy, but an international policy, and responsibility for its enforcement rests not on the United States alone but on all nine parties to the treaty.

The agenda or program of the Conference offered as one of the subjects to be considered the status of existing commitments in China. When Secretary Hughes brought this subject up before the Far Eastern Committee, Japan entered an emphatic objection to its consideration, and the matter was dropped immediately without argument. The treaty, therefore, is not retroactive, for it recognizes the status quo in Manchuria and to a less extent in other parts of China. The saving clause of the new agreement is, however, a resolution providing for the establishment of an international board of reference, to which questions arising in regard to the open door may be referred.

Will Japan respect the pledges she has made and live up to the spirit of her promises? If she does, the Washington Conference will prove to be a great success. If, on the contrary, Japan does not intend to live up to her pledges or intends to fulfill them only in part, her position in Asia has been greatly strengthened. She is more firmly intrenched in Manchuria than ever. She holds the Maritime Province of Siberia under a promise to get out, which she has repeatedly made and repeatedly broken, as was plainly stated by Secretary Hughes before the full Committee on Far Eastern Affairs, and repeated at a plenary session of the Conference. His statement was one of the most remarkable, by reason of its directness and unvarnished truth, in the history of American diplomacy. After reviewing the correspondence between the two governments and the reiterated assurances of Japan of her intention to withdraw from Siberia, assurances which so far had not been carried out, Mr. Hughes expressed his gratification at the renewal of these assurances before the Conference in plenary session. Unless Japan is utterly devoid of moral shame, she will have to make good her word this time.

When the treaties drafted by the Conference were submitted by the President to the Senate, they encountered serious opposition, but were finally ratified. The Republican leaders, particularly Senator Lodge, were twitted with charges of inconsistency in advocating certain features of these treaties when they had violently opposed the League of Nations. The Four-Power Treaty is much more of an entangling alliance than the Covenant of the League, and the Naval Treaty deprives Congress for a period of fifteen years of its constitutional right to determine the size of the navy and to provide for the defense of Guam and the Philippines. In fact, there were very few objections raised to the League of Nations which could not with equal force be applied to the Four-Power and Naval Treaties. The Four-Power Treaty was the main object of attack, and Senators Lodge and Underwood were greatly embarrassed in attempting to explain its meaning. Its "baffling brevity" demanded explanations, but no satisfactory explanations were forthcoming. They talked in general terms about the tremendous importance of the treaty, but they dared not state the real fact that the treaty was drafted by Mr. Balfour and Baron Kato as the most convenient method of terminating the Anglo-Japanese Alliance without making it appear to the Japanese public that their government had surrendered the alliance without due compensation. According to an Associated Press Dispatch from Tokio, January 31, 1922, Baron Uchida, the Japanese Minister of Foreign Affairs, replying to interpolations in the House of Peers, said: "The Four-Power Treaty was not intended to abrogate the Anglo-Japanese Alliance, but rather to widen and extend it." The real *quid pro quo* for the termination of the Anglo-Japanese Alliance was the agreement of the United States not to construct naval bases or new fortifications in Guam and the Philippines, and the clause terminating the Anglo-Japanese Alliance might just as well have been attached to the Naval

Treaty, but this would not have satisfied Japanese public opinion. Great Britain and Japan were permitted to terminate their alliance in any way that they might deem best. After the Four-Power Treaty was accepted by the American delegates, they feared that it would look too much as if the United States had merely been drawn into the Anglo-Japanese Alliance. It was decided, therefore, at the eleventh hour to give the agreement a more general character by inviting France to adhere to it. France agreed to sign, although she resented not having been consulted during the negotiation of the treaty.

The achievements of the Conference, although falling far short of the extravagant claims made by the President and the American delegates, are undoubtedly of great importance. The actual scrapping of millions of dollars' worth of ships in commission or in process of construction gives the world an object lesson such as it has never had before. One of the most significant results of the Conference was the development of a complete accord between England and the United States, made possible by the settlement of the Irish question and furthered by the tact and gracious bearing of Mr. Balfour. One of the unfortunate results was the increased isolation of France, due to the failure of her delegates to grasp the essential elements of the situation and to play any but a negative role. The success of the Conference was due largely to Secretary Hughes who, though handicapped at every point by fear of the Senate and by the unfortunate commitments of President Harding during the last campaign, may be said on the whole to have played his hand reasonably well.

Meanwhile we are still drifting, so far as a general European policy is concerned. President Harding's idea of holding aloof from "Europe's league," as he prefers to designate the League of Nations, and of having a little league of our own in the Pacific, will not work. The world's problems cannot be segregated in this way. Europe's league includes all of the principal American nations except the United States and Mexico, while our Pacific league includes the two leading European powers. As soon as the American people realize—and there are indications that they are already waking up to the reality—that the depression in domestic industry and foreign commerce is due to conditions in Europe and that prosperity will not return until we take a hand in the solution of European problems, there will be a general demand for a constructive policy and America will no longer hesitate to reassume the leadership which she renounced in the referendum of 1920, but which the rest of the world is ready to accord to her again.

CPSIA information can be obtained
at www.ICGtesting.com
Printed in the USA
BVHW021151020523
663429BV00012B/311